This twenty-one-d[...] against the chains that keep people bound to arrested development! If you're struggling to get free or stay free, *read this book!*

—ALEXANDER PAGANI
BEST-SELLING AUTHOR OF *THE SECRETS TO DELIVERANCE* AND *THE SECRETS TO GENERATIONAL CURSES*

I love this book! *Prison Break* isn't just about breaking physical barriers; it's about demolishing the mental, emotional, and spiritual shackles that have so many people bound. Having walked his own journey from incarceration to freedom through Christ, Pastor Juan Martinez shows us how to break every chain, including the limiting beliefs and behaviors that keep us from being all God called us to be.

When His mercy meets our mess, everything changes. No matter what has you trapped—whether it's past trauma, negative thinking, or even dead religion—this book offers a ray of hope. *Prison Break* is more than a devotional; it's a lifeline to healing and restoration in every part of your life. Whom the Son sets free is free indeed!

—REAL TALK KIM

Pastor Juan's guidance has helped me in life because he brings the full counsel of the Lord. His passion for people is contagious, and he brings an authenticity to the Christian space that is much needed.

—GRANT STUARD
LINEBACKER, INDIANAPOLIS COLTS

Pastor Juan Martinez's testimony has captivated over 150,000 viewers worldwide on our network, encouraging and challenging thousands to seek a deeper relationship with God. Yet what has moved me the most is witnessing firsthand Pastor Juan's profound love and unwavering commitment to liberating souls from spiritual chains. There's no doubt in my mind that this book, in the name of Jesus, will do just that!

—ERIC VILLATORO
EXECUTIVE DIRECTOR, DELAFÉ TESTIMONIES

My good friend Pastor Juan Martinez has the unique ability to share deep spiritual insights in a relaxed, conversational way. Juan's humility and love for God's people shines through in everything he does. His great sense of humor and larger-than-life personality enable him to share the keys he has learned during his miraculous journey with God from prison to the pulpit in a relatable way.

—JEREMY COE
COFOUNDER, *REAL VIDA TV*

My friend Juan Martinez is a phenomenal leader, an incredible pastor, and a great example of a family man and Spirit-filled believer. If you ever get the chance to meet Juan, you will love him immediately. He practices what he preaches, and in his newest book, *Prison Break*, he gives you the tools he has applied in his own life to bring lasting breakthrough. This book is an absolute must-read!

—EVANGELIST DON BABIN

What can I say to let you know how much you need this book? Juan Martinez shows you as a reader how your mindsets, beliefs, and accepted reality are indeed your prison cell. It's not the world around you that has locked you in these bars; it's what is inside you. Find out how you can break through these barriers in twenty-one days. Three weeks will change the rest of your life! This is a book written from a firsthand and real perspective to help you grow and change.

—PASTOR CALEB RING
RIVER CLERMONT CHURCH

Prison Break is not just a gripping read; it's a testament to the power of redemption and freedom. Through the pages of this compelling book, readers will journey alongside a remarkable man driven by a deep desire to see others set free.

Rooted in faith and fueled by compassion, Pastor Juan exemplifies the transformative power of Jesus, offering hope to those in the darkest of circumstances. This book is a must-read for anyone seeking inspiration and wanting to experience the truth that no chains are too strong to be broken.

—Zee

Artist, Kingdom Muzic

I'm a big believer in the saying, "You cannot give what you do not have, and you cannot transfer what you have not held." Over the past decade I have seen Pastor Juan live the life that he preaches behind closed doors—modeling the principles he teaches in this book in his marriage, family, and leadership. Pastor Juan has walked the steps to freedom he shares in this book. So many people aren't in physical chains yet live in bondage every day, and we have seen so many people who are in physical chains set free from all of their bondage. *Prison Break* is for anyone who is ready to experience true spiritual and mental freedom.

—Pastor Rey Sandoval

Rise Church

Prison Break is a great tool to help you go through your day-to-day life. Pastor Juan has again incorporated his real-life situations and experiences to help us understand that God is faithful, and no matter who you are, you will face decisions that can determine your future. One of the most unique ways to learn is from one another's experiences, and this devotional allows you to learn from Pastor Juan, thanks to his transparency, truth, and love. Not only do I challenge you to take on this devotional but also to share it with someone else. Thank you, Juan, for another great way to display the love of Christ.

—Vinny De Leon
Pastor, Get Wrapped Church
Owner, Vinny's Barbershop and Peak
Performance Mentorship

Pastor Juan has been my spiritual father, pastor, and friend for over ten years. His testimony of overcoming and breaking free from an incarcerated mindset has been a prime example of what a godly person looks like. He walks the walk, and his fruit is evident. His life is an example and encouragement to the Get Wrapped Church congregation, his family, and those around him. He is *real*. *Prison Break* is full of captivating truth and bold honesty—a powerfully unique delivery accompanied by life experience and humility. Get ready to see the chains break off your life!

—Megan McCullum
President, Heels To Halos

PRISON
BREAK

JUAN MARTINEZ

CHARISMA
HOUSE

While the author has made every effort to provide accurate, up-to-date source information at the time of publication, statistics and other data are constantly updated. Neither the

For more resources like this, visit MyCharismaShop.com and the author's website at Juanmartinez.tv.

Cataloging-in-Publication Data is on file with the Library of Congress.
International Standard Book Number: 978-1-63641-387-7
E-book ISBN: 978-1-63641-388-4

1 2024
Printed in the United States of America

Most Charisma Media products are available at special quantity discounts for bulk purchase for sales promotions, premiums, fund-raising, and educational needs. For details, call us at (407) 333-0600 or visit our website at charismamedia.com.

I dedicate this book to every person who has walked out of prison and not gone back—both those who have been behind physical prison walls and those who have accepted Jesus as their Lord and Savior and allowed the power of the gospel of Jesus Christ to set them free and now go into the highways and byways with the keys to liberate others.

May this book remind us where we have come from and give us a clear understanding of our mission to set the captives free! May we all say, "Send me; I'll go." Thank You, Lord, for setting us free.

CONTENTS

FOREWORD

THIS IS AN amazing book—one for today and tomorrow. Timeless, powerful, and anointed, *Prison Break* offers revelation and clarity about how we should walk, live, and honor the Lord Jesus Christ by having the mind of Christ.

When I think of a "prison break," I think of people like my friend David Berkowitz. I am struck by how this precious brother could be physically incarcerated and yet free in his mind. You may know the story of Brother David, formerly known as the Son of Sam. He once worshipped demons and has been sentenced to six consecutive life sentences for the crimes he committed. Yet as I have visited him, prayed with him, and done Bible studies in prison with him, I have never met anyone freer in his spirit, mind, and soul. Even while behind bars he has led thousands of people to the Lord Jesus Christ.

God's power can set people free no matter what had them bound. In this incredible book, Dr. Juan Martinez teaches you how to fight the good fight of faith in your mind, heart, spirit, and soul so you can walk in truth and freedom and honor the Lord Jesus Christ on the battlefield today and tomorrow. It's time to be armed and dangerous.

What Juan addresses in these pages reminds me of when the apostle Paul was standing trial before the Roman governor Festus and Israel's King Agrippa and boldly testified of how the Lord Jesus Christ appeared to him in a vision and transformed his life. Although Paul was in shackles physically, he was free spiritually. Festus and Agrippa were not in chains physically, but they were spiritually incarcerated. What a powerful testimony of what it means to be free indeed!

Juan is a gift to the body of Christ. He's the real deal who has allowed the gospel of Jesus Christ to transform his life and now wants everyone to experience the same love that changed him.

Prison Break was written for a time such as this to set the captives free so they can stand in the face of adversity and be used as a weapon in the hands of a mighty God against the kingdom of darkness. It's time to fight, and it's time to win.

It's time to get free!

—JOHN RAMIREZ
INTERNATIONAL EVANGELIST
AUTHOR, *FIRE PRAYERS* AND *UNMASKING THE DEVIL*

ACKNOWLEDGMENTS

I WANT TO START by thanking my beautiful wife, Ruthy—my Baby Ruth. You have always believed in me and stood with me through all the stressful and crazy days. Thank you for loving me the way you do and for always reminding me that I was made for greatness.

To all my kiddos—Nina, Jonathan, Jay, Josh, Valery, and Johnathan—thank you for always believing in me. I'm grateful God has made me dad to the greatest kiddos in the world.

Vinny and Sara, thank you for always believing in me and the vision God has given us to build the kingdom. No matter what season we've been in, you guys have been there.

Get Wrapped Church, you guys are a "that's crazy; no, that's God" people, and I want to thank you for your prayers and for always believing in the impossible.

Pastors Todd, Stephanie, Tanya, and Megan, you guys have worked so hard at holding my arms up. Thank you.

Gateway Church—all I can say is wow, wow, wow. Thank you for the wise counsel. Pastor David Vestal, you're a champ. Who would have thought God would give me a narcotics detective as a mentor!

John Ramirez, as you would say, "Brothaaaaaaaaa!" Thank you for sticking with me like white on rice. I appreciate and love you for staying on me about writing a book. Now we can say I've written *books*.

Gregg and Michelle Lucas, thank you for always pushing me to do great things.

I also want to honor my spiritual parents, Billy and Vinnie Yarborough. You guys have been Jesus walking the earth. Mama Vinnie, you always believed in me and spoke things to me that brought me comfort and thrust me forward. Billy, I miss you, but I know you would be proud.

I want to thank Mary Ann Soliz, Iron Sharpens Iron, and Gerardo and Krystal for your continued love and support.

Finally, to my mom, Elsa, thank you for always praying and never giving up on the promises of God for me. You are my hero. (*Gracias, Mami, por siempre orar por mi y nunca renunciar a las promesas de Dios. Tú eres mi héroe.*)

INTRODUCTION

WHEN MOST PEOPLE think about jail or prison, television is their only point of reference. I can tell you that is not the reality. While some TV shows and movies capture the appearance of correctional facilities, they don't convey the despair and darkness inside the walls. You have to step inside to experience that.

The thing that might surprise you, though, is how many inmates return once they are freed. According to the Bureau of Justice Statistics, roughly two-thirds (66 percent) of prisoners released across twenty-four states in 2008 were arrested again within three years, and 82 percent were arrested within ten years of their release.[1]

That trend isn't limited to the twenty-four states in the study. Whenever I lead prison ministry, I ask the inmates how many of them have been incarcerated before. Surprisingly, almost everyone raises their hands. I promise you, it's at least 98 percent every time.

Then I will ask how many have been locked up twice. Nearly all the hands go up again. Next I ask how many have been incarcerated four or five times. Again, most of the hands go up.

After that, I ask another series of questions: "How many of you were raised right? How many of you grew up going to church? How many of you have someone in your life who is sad or hurt that you are locked up in here?" Again, most of the hands go up.

From the many times I have done this icebreaker, I reasoned

that a history of incarceration does not prevent a person from returning to prison, and those who came from good homes and even people who were raised in church could end up behind bars. Some inmates are really good people who chose to do the wrong thing. Being raised in single-parent homes contributes to this a lot.

After making this observation, I began to approach prison ministry differently. I started telling guys that instead of thinking of their parole papers or the exit door as their freedom, they needed to get free mentally first so they could stay free physically. And dudes would almost always say, "Yo, Pastor Juan, whatcha mean?"

I would then break down my story for them. I let them know that I have been out of prison for fifteen years, and I have stayed out. I often tell inmates the reason they are incarcerated is that *they were already incarcerated*. Before they landed behind bars, they were already locked up mentally.

At first everyone looks confused, but then I say one thing and watch the light bulbs go on in their minds: "If you are going to stay free out there, you've got to get free while you are still in here."

Here's an example of what I mean. I live in Houston, and to get to Dallas from my house, you always take I-45 north. If someone wants to go to Dallas and gets on I-45 south, they'll just get frustrated because they'll wind up in downtown Houston. At some point they're going to have to change direction so they can get where they want to go.

It has been said that doing the same thing and expecting a different result is insanity. What do you think?

I once read a Chinese proverb that said, "Always follow a man who is on his way back to where you want to be." I'm hoping you will give an ear to someone who was once incarcerated physically because he was incarcerated mentally but has been liberated by the power of the Holy Spirit.

Over and over, I've seen people exit the prison door only to wind up back in the same place. The difference between them and the inmates who get free and stay free is what happens before they leave the prison yard.

Back when I was in the prison system, people would tell me, "Yo, Martinez, like, tone it down! You are way too happy. We are locked up!" But I would tell them, "I'm not in prison. I'm in *college*. I'm only here till I graduate." They thought I was nuts, but having that positive mentality made all the difference. I would remind myself daily, "This is just a season I'm going through [my wilderness] to find out who I really am. Jesus is setting me free."

As a result, when I was released from prison, I never went back. And I kicked all the other habits I practiced because of my incarcerated mentality. I haven't gotten high; I haven't cheated; I haven't watched porn. I love my wife, I'm a father to my children, and I finally understand friendships and relationships. I'm a son of the King, and I'm free now in every way!

IT'S NOT OVER!

As a pastor, I often remind others that they don't have to be chained to their past. If you were (or are) incarcerated, God can still redeem your life. There is more to your story, so don't live in that one negative moment and let it define your entire existence. God gave His only Son so we all might have "life, and…have it more abundantly" (John 10:10, MEV).

I love that God is no respecter of persons. Interestingly enough, neither is the enemy of our souls. Nothing shows the torment of the entire human race like the US prison system. People of all nationalities, ethnicities, and social statuses are represented there. While serving, I encountered prisoners from all types of backgrounds. Though we didn't grow up together, we all shared a commonality: pain and trauma. Even the toughest, biggest, most hard-core prisoners wanted to be free. We all wished we had less time behind bars.

Every inmate has looked at the barbed-wire fences and thought of escaping at least once. We would look at the beautiful blue skies, feel the sunshine hitting our faces, and not be able to go out and enjoy everything God created—not because of God but because we were incarcerated!

Even if you've never been incarcerated, maybe you can relate to feeling alone, feeling like you'll never get out of your circumstances, or looking at people full of joy and not experiencing that happiness. In other words, maybe you feel just like we did looking at the barbed-wire fences. You're actually out in the world, yet you feel incarcerated. You may be struggling with addiction, unforgiveness, guilt, shame, pride, fear, anxiety, or anger. Or maybe you just feel stuck in life.

No matter what has you bound, freedom is available to you. God still loves you. He doesn't view you based on your shortcomings. Take it from me. While I was still incarcerated, I wound up meeting Jesus. Through Him, I found freedom. No one is perfect. In God's eyes, we have all committed a crime. We all have sinned and come short of His glory. We are all guilty. But through Christ we can be forgiven, and our sins can be washed clean.

I spent twenty-three years behind the bars life had placed around my mind and heart. I spent ten of those years inside prison walls and the rest running from God. I was lost. But after I got saved in prison, I met my beautiful wife (my Baby Ruth) and eventually became a pastor. God restored my relationship with my kiddos, and I gained three more kiddos. (Well, they are adults now, but they are still my kiddos.)

Soon I started meeting influential people. God fast-tracked me in ministry. I ultimately wound up on the radio and became a host on TBN Salsa and other television outlets. All of these opportunities opened doors for me. I also earned a doctoral degree and have ministered around the country and internationally. I say all this so you will know that no matter what has you bound, your life is not over. It is still possible for you to experience whatever God has for you.

My relationship with Jesus enabled me to be a light in any room. I learned how to use the darkness I had overcome to testify to God's goodness. I learned how to encourage others who had experienced the same traumas I endured. According to 1 Peter 3, God has given us everything we need for life and godliness. Though most people see me as a confident person, in reality I'm not. Instead, I crucify my flesh and allow the Spirit of God to empower me and help me move in a direction that brings Him glory.

The truth is that over my lifetime I've spent more time getting high than serving Jesus. I've made many mistakes, but rather than shrink back like a coward, I press forward with my testimony. Even when I feel unworthy I keep the faith because I know God is getting the glory. This is why I tell my story; it is why I earned my doctorate and decided to write books. I want to share the gospel with as many people as God allows. I want to help people be released from the prison of fear, addiction, or whatever else they may be struggling with.

Even though I've talked about my incarceration, I'm not writing this book solely for people who are behind bars. My goal is to reach those in the body of Christ who are incarcerated mentally and spiritually. They talk like they are free, but they don't bear any fruit. You can see they are still imprisoned. How do I know? I know what imprisonment looks like. Many believers follow "Churchianity" and not Christianity. They go to church but are not followers of Jesus Christ. Those people may be bound mentally, locked up emotionally, and possibly not even saved yet.

I want everyone to realize that Jesus loves them. The Father is available to all, and everyone is welcome at the table. His arms are always open.

Think about it like this: When you're lost, you lean on a GPS, right? Similarly, if you're lost spiritually, God wants you to lean on Him. You don't have to fall back on plan B with God because He is reliable. He will always get you where you need to be. That's why I follow Jesus. If heaven is my destination, all I have to do is follow Him.

Although I'm imperfect and have flaws, I've allowed Jesus to apprehend my heart. A formerly incarcerated person understands what it's like to be captured. The difference is that when the Holy Spirit apprehends us, we experience freedom instead of bondage.

WALK THE YELLOW LINE

In the prison yard, they had painted these yellow lines we were supposed to use when we went from place to place. There were almost two thousand men, and no one really walked the lines. One day the Lord said to me, "You need to walk the line." Because of my love for Him, I started to follow the rules. People would yell at me, "Hey, New York! What are you doing over there?" I was the only guy walking the line while everyone else was all over the place.

I was the only guy! Do you understand what I'm saying?

I remember being embarrassed about it, and when people asked me what I was doing, I didn't want to tell them it was because God told me to do it. I was still in my pride, but I walked the line regardless. While walking the lines, God would talk to me about walking the narrow road. He shared with me that if I couldn't change my life in the little things, I would never do it in the big things. If I was going to stay out of prison, I would have to change in the little ways. God showed me a picture of the world and how broad the path is that leads to destruction.

The world didn't want to walk the line, but I was called to, in hope that others would eventually follow the narrow path too. In time, guys I was going to church with began walking next to me. They would ask, "Why are you doing this?" And I would respond, "Because God told me that if I didn't do this, I would never change." That's when other men joined me. Four became seven, seven became eleven, and eleven became an entire group of people walking the yellow line. It was super dope because these like-minded men wanted to change for the better.

During that time, God revealed to me that shortcuts are actually long-cuts. When I cut corners with my money, responsibilities, and relationships, I usually end up making mistakes and having to repeat steps. I have to fix whatever I rushed through because I did not take the time to do it right the first time. The same is true with our lives in general. If you take a shortcut, you might have to redo it thirty times and spend five years accomplishing what should have taken months. Instead, God wants us to do the little things right the first time.

Confronting the thing you're struggling with is not just about your freedom; anybody connected to you will also benefit. God's palace is way cooler than slavery. Therefore, we should allow the Holy Spirit to do what He does best: break bondages so we can experience God's freedom.

In each day of this twenty-one-day journey I include some teaching that will help you identify a truth that could lead you to greater freedom. Then I include a Spiritual Freedom Study, where I challenge you to meditate on Scripture and respond to some questions so you'll start to recognize what you do and don't believe—and how you can change. Each day also includes a prayer and what I call Listening Time, when you allow the Holy Spirit to speak to you. Talking is great, but if we don't listen to God, we're not really communicating with Him.

I designed this book to be interactive, so you'll find space to respond and reflect. But if you need more room to write, feel free to grab a journal or notebook. Do whatever you need to do!

Before you begin, I want you to pray. Ask the Holy Spirit for revelation of the truth, and posture your heart in a place of humility. Humbling ourselves is always the first step to change. As long as you keep defending your dysfunctional behavior, you will not experience deliverance. Let the Holy Spirit guide you, and don't forget to enjoy the journey.

Say it with me: "My life will never be the same, in Jesus' name!"

BREAK FREE FROM RELIGION

ONE ADVANTAGE OF being a pastor who comes from the streets is that I can easily spot people who have an addiction, including in the church. Let's just say my discernment muscle has been well trained. Now, I'm not talking about people addicted to heroin or cocaine. Nope. I'm talking about those who use church like a drug. These are people who go to church and scream, holler, and feel God in the moment but are incapable or unwilling to develop a genuine relationship with Him.

Let me be clear: Relationships are complex, whether with fellow human beings or God. It's much easier to distill religion into a rule book or debate strategy than to really get to know God. But no matter how hard people try, they can't transform their religious knowledge into a relationship that produces Holy Spirit power. Religion may seem to have all the answers, but it often fails to recognize the true power of God. It is not enough to go through the motions and pretend to have a relationship with God. That's why one of the first steps in breaking free of whatever has us trapped is to let go of religion and actually connect with God.

To truly connect with God, we must make a lifelong commitment to Him, much like in a marriage. If there's no cross,

1

there's no power. The power we need to break free of the chains that have us bound is at the cross. When we put away our foolish ways, we will see the fruit of repentance. We can't just do good things and expect goodness to follow. We can read our Bibles, pray, and fast—all good stuff—but we have nothing if we are not in relationship with God. He doesn't just want to be first in our lives; He wants to be our everything.

We may want to walk in the power of God, but we have to get to know God to understand how He moves. This happens when we crucify our own will and desires and put Him first in our daily choices. When we release our manipulative ways and allow ourselves to be led by His Spirit into truth, we experience His power.

One day while I was praying, I sensed the Lord saying, "Juan, you know, you guys are doing it wrong." And I thought, "What?" Then He said, "Shout it from the rooftops: *You gotta have a relationship with Jesus Christ.*" I have visited churches both in the United States and abroad where Christians talked about having a relationship with Jesus everywhere they went. But the Lord told me, "Juan, My people don't understand the word *relationship.*"

God kept downloading revelation to me, and another time He said, "Some who have received salvation think they have a relationship with Me. Yet they don't because they never had a relationship with their earthly father or haven't seen a good example of a mother and father."

This hit me like a ton of bricks because I had a rocky childhood relationship with my father. I knew a father provided for his kids, but my idea of a father was nowhere near the image God wanted me to have of Him. If a person has never seen a healthy father figure or has never been in a healthy relationship, how are they supposed to know how to build a deep relationship with God?

This is the problem we see in the church. Many people gravitate toward religious traditions and go to church seeking an emotional high because they don't know how to have a personal relationship with Jesus. They don't know how to communicate and connect with Him because they've never actually seen a healthy relationship.

Growing up, I saw my dad only once a month. He never communicated with me the way I've learned to talk to my wife and kids. I don't just speak to be heard or refuse to listen to anybody else. I don't tell my family or anyone else that what they say doesn't matter. *I communicate.*

Before I became a Christian, I didn't know how to communicate. I didn't know how to love my wife well or even what the word *relationship* actually meant. Learning to communicate was hard at first because I wasn't looking to Jesus or trying to listen to Him. Instead, I just told Him what I needed and kept rolling. Coming from Catholicism, I might have said a Hail Mary, but I didn't know if God would answer, though I was hopeful.

Looking back, I realize I had no real relationship or communication with God, even though I thought I did. When I eventually began to understand what having a relationship with Christ truly meant, that's when my heart shifted.

One definition of the word *relationship* is "the way in which two or more concepts, objects, or people are connected, or the state of being connected."[1] A relationship is also defined as "the state of being connected by blood or marriage" and "the way in which two or more people or groups regard and behave toward each other."[2]

The latter explanation is most captivating. It reminds me of the relationship between a landlord and tenant. Each party in that relationship has a role and responsibility, right? That means understanding our roles helps us create a better connection.

For example, the landlord must maintain the place where the tenant lives. And the tenant has to pay the rent, lease, or whatever they've promised to give the landlord. If either party fails to properly connect according to their roles, *boom*—the entire relationship blows up!

From here I started thinking about the whole construct of parent-child and husband-wife relationships. After I got saved and was later released from prison, I set out to rebuild my relationship with my children, whom I had not seen in nineteen years because I was touring as a drug dealer, serving the devil. I was like, "What up! I'm Dad." And they were like, "What up! I'm son [or daughter]." Even though we had titles, I had to learn how to be a father, and they had to discover their roles as my children in order for us to have a relationship. It took about eight years to do so, but we finally connected once we understood our roles.

Connecting differs from speaking. Everyone talks, but few connect. My children and I talked so we could connect. We listened not just to the other person's words but also to their heart. We communicated. I am their father, they are my kids, and when we finally connected, we operated as such. We struggled at first, though, because we had never experienced the kind of connection I wanted us to have. Sometimes I would get so frustrated because there I was, the dad, begging my kids,

"Yo, text me back! Communication goes both ways. I can't do all the texting." But then the Lord revealed to me, "You expect them to do something they've never done with you just because you're their father." When God said that, I thought, "Oh, man."

Our relationship with God grows as we communicate with Him. Communication draws us into a deeper connection.

To love God means actively doing what He prefers. It means embracing His will, choosing what He desires, and obeying His Word. We do not show God love when we put Him on the back end. When we say, "Oh, I messed up; I'm sorry," but continue to do what we want, that is not love; that is manipulation. Love is designed to help you control your emotions and choose what God prefers—that's how you mature. You develop and evolve every time you love. And here's the crazy part: When I choose what God prefers, that choice always wins.

Many speak "Christianese" and say they're going to "die daily" but they never do, so nothing happens. We must live by the truth. When we reject our way and choose God's preferred way instead, our religious knowledge is transformed into a power-packed, God-filled relationship that empowers us to connect with Him and others!

SPIRITUAL FREEDOM STUDY

> For the word of the cross is foolishness to those who are perishing, but it is the power of God to us who are being saved.
>
> —1 Corinthians 1:18, csb

If there's no cross, there's no power. Without the cross we can't connect to Jesus and develop a relationship with Him. If we want to experience God's power to set us free, we must choose knowing Jesus personally over following a list of religious dos and don'ts. Nothing we do can make us righteous before God—not even good things like Bible study, prayer, and going to church can save us. Only accepting what Jesus did for us on the cross and choosing His will over our own can lead us into the abundant life Christ died for us to have.

If you haven't made Jesus your Lord, go to the appendix to learn how to know Jesus. That is truly the first step to breaking free of your personal prisons. Then commit to being in a relationship with Him. Instead of just going through the religious motions, truly communicate with Him. Pray and then listen for His response, and commit to obeying what He says.

Questions for Reflection

Do you find yourself focusing on fulfilling religious duties instead of spending time getting to know God? If so, why? If not, how did you avoid that trap?

_____

_____

How might shifting from a religious mindset to a relationship mindset impact the way believers approach prayer and spiritual practices?

_____

_____

What changes do you need to make in order to better connect with God and focus on building a relationship with Him instead of fulfilling religious duties or just going through the motions?

_____

_____

Prayer Time (Talk to Him)

> *Heavenly Father, I come before You today with an open heart and a sincere desire to know You more intimately. I acknowledge that I want more than religious routines; I want a genuine relationship with You. In Jesus' name, amen.*

Listening Time

Now pray, "Holy Spirit, what are You saying to me?" Use the space provided, or a journal or notebook, to write what He reveals to you.

_____

_____

Begin to know Him now, and finish never.
—OSWALD CHAMBERS

THE PRICE OF FREEDOM

I RECENTLY WATCHED A movie called *The Burial*. It is loosely based on the true story of lawyer Willie E. Gary and his client, funeral home owner Jeremiah "Jerry" O'Keefe. Facing financial troubles, O'Keefe entered into a contract with a large funeral home company owned by Raymond Loewen. But when Loewen didn't follow through on their agreement, O'Keefe suspected that Loewen was intentionally trying to force him into bankruptcy to snatch up his entire business.

The movie takes you on an emotional roller coaster, and in the end (spoiler alert) O'Keefe was awarded $500 million in damages—and that was in 1995 dollars.[1]

I bring up this film because it parallels how the enemy of our souls works against us. Satan seeks to exploit God's children and make us spiritually, emotionally, mentally, physically, and financially bankrupt. He comes to us with a solution we think will solve all our problems, but in the end it leaves us on the brink of losing it all! The devil comes to kill, steal, and destroy each and every one of us. No one is exempt.

But like O'Keefe, you can overcome—because you have the right defender. O'Keefe had a flashy lawyer named Willie Gary. You have God in heaven. He looked down thousands of years ago and knew you and I would face a formidable foe. For this reason, He loved us all so much that He sent His only begotten Son to the world to atone for our sins.

This is the crux of the gospel, something you likely have heard if you've accepted Jesus as your Savior. But I'm focusing on it today because one reason so many people are not representing the kingdom of God and living victoriously in Christ is that they have lost sight of the cross. They have a form of godliness but deny its power.

The cross is more than a charm we wear to represent our risen Savior. The cross is the place where we received eternal victory over death, hell, and the grave. First Corinthians 6:20 says, "You were bought at a price. Therefore honor God with your bodies."

The reason so many Christians are not representing the kingdom of God and living victoriously is that they have lost sight of the cross. Many have held to a form of godliness but have denied its power.

Today we will look at passages from Luke 23. We'll see the power of what Jesus endured for our sins and learn how to endure seasons of trial by observing the way Jesus endured His.

Let's begin in verses 1–3 (NLT):

> Then the entire council took Jesus to Pilate, the Roman governor. They began to state their case: "This man has been leading our people astray by telling them not to pay their taxes to the Roman government and by claiming he is the Messiah, a king."

> So Pilate asked him, "Are you the king of the Jews?"
>
> Jesus replied, "You have said it."

First, we must keep in mind that Jesus knew no sin. He had done nothing wrong. Yet He was being accused of leading people astray and instructing Jews not to pay taxes to Rome. We know Jesus told the people to "give to Caesar what belongs to Caesar, and give to God what belongs to God" (Mark 12:17, NLT). Yet the council claimed Jesus did the opposite.

Let this remind us that sometimes we can be doing good— telling the truth, helping people, minding our business—and still run into trouble. When that happens, understand that God is preparing you for a victory you can't quite see yet.

Next, notice that Jesus' response was to the point. He simply replied, "You have said it." He was a verbal tactician. He was cool under pressure and said only what was necessary. We often get ourselves in trouble by giving people a piece of our minds and reacting emotionally. But remember, we mature spiritually when we choose what God wants. When the flesh dies, the spirit lives.

In Luke 23:4 we see that Pilate found nothing wrong with Jesus, but the noise from the religious leaders and the crowd only intensified. So Pilate found a loophole to send Jesus to another official. Let this also be a lesson for us. It is hard to stand firm on your convictions if the crowd can sway you. We must put pleasing God over pleasing people.

When Pilate learned that Jesus was from Galilee, he sent Him to the official in that jurisdiction, Herod. Interestingly, even though Herod mocked Jesus, he secretly wanted to encounter Jesus and see Him perform a miracle. Although Herod plied Him with questions, Jesus said nothing. Still under pressure from the crowd, Herod let the chief priests and religious leaders accuse Jesus. Then he and his soldiers mocked and ridiculed Him. But Herod couldn't find any fault in Jesus either, so he sent Him back to Pilate.

The Bible tells us Herod and Pilate had been enemies, but they became friends that day, and they stood in agreement that Jesus was not guilty of what the crowd accused Him of doing (Luke 23:12–13). This tells me we can never underestimate how God may use an unfavorable season to correct a situation or produce a positive result for someone else. He can use things that might seem horrible for our good.

Yet even after Herod and Pilate gave their verdicts, the masses cried, "Crucify Him!" This revealed to me that sometimes the people we help will accuse us of wrongdoing. We cannot let that stop us from doing the Lord's work, but we must understand the risk and proceed with wisdom.

Undeterred by Herod and Pilate, the masses called for the officials to release an actual criminal named Barabbas and execute Jesus instead. Unlike O'Keefe in the movie, Jesus did not have an attorney advocating on His behalf. There was no plea bargaining with the district attorney. There was no time to file an appeal with the judge. It seemed as though Jesus' fate was sealed.

In a moment of vulnerability Jesus had asked His Father in heaven if He could be spared the cup of this affliction. This showed Jesus' humanity. Yet He prayed, "Not My will, but Yours, be done" (Luke 22:42, NKJV). Jesus chose surrender before His trial. And when the rubber met the road and

He was in the midst of all that pain, Jesus still chose God's will, His Father's preferred choice. This is what the cross represents for you and me—dying to self and choosing what pleases God. If Jesus the Son of God had to die to His will, so must we!

After being beaten and hung between two criminals, Jesus took His last breath and was buried in a borrowed tomb. If this were a movie, it would seem all was lost and the haters had won. But that was not the end of the story. In Luke 24 we read about Jesus' glorious resurrection, and in verses 44–53 (NLT) Jesus revealed Himself to His disciples before ascending to heaven.

> Then he said, "When I was with you before, I told you that everything written about me in the law of Moses and the prophets and in the Psalms must be fulfilled." Then he opened their minds to understand the Scriptures. And he said, "Yes, it was written long ago that the Messiah would suffer and die and rise from the dead on the third day. It was also written that this message would be proclaimed in the authority of his name to all the nations, beginning in Jerusalem: 'There is forgiveness of sins for all who repent.' You are witnesses of all these things. And now I will send the Holy Spirit, just as my Father promised. But stay here in the city until the Holy Spirit comes and fills you with power from heaven."
>
> Then Jesus led them to Bethany, and lifting his hands to heaven, he blessed them. While he was

blessing them, he left them and was taken up to
heaven. So they worshiped him and then returned
to Jerusalem filled with great joy. And they spent
all of their time in the Temple, praising God.

Jesus became poor so we can become rich in God. He
willingly paid the price for our sins because of His love for you
and me. Let us show that same love to others so we can make
Christ known everywhere we go. We do this not by might nor
by power but by His Spirit!

Living in victory brings glory to the One who paid the price
for our freedom. Remember, "it is for freedom that Christ has
set us free" (Gal. 5:1).

SPIRITUAL FREEDOM STUDY

Read the following scriptures:

> I have been crucified with Christ and I no longer
> live, but Christ lives in me. The life I now live in
> the body, I live by faith in the Son of God, who
> loved me and gave himself for me.
>
> —GALATIANS 2:20, NIV

> And whoever doesn't take up his cross and follow
> me is not worthy of me. Anyone who finds his life
> will lose it, and anyone who loses his life because
> of me will find it.
>
> —MATTHEW 10:38–39, CSB

Take a moment to reflect on the price Jesus paid for your freedom. I would also encourage you to read Luke 23 and 24 in their entirety when you get some free time.

Questions for Reflection

Focusing on Matthew 10:38–39 and Galatians 2:20, what stands out about the power of the cross?

_____

_____

Are you living for yourself, or have you taken up your cross? How can you die to your ways and activate the supernatural power of the cross in your life?

_____

_____

Prayer Time (Talk to Him)

> *Heavenly Father, thank You for the immeasurable love You displayed at the cross for me. Ignite a fire within me to live a life that brings You glory, that at the cross others may find freedom. May Your kingdom come and Your will be done. In Jesus' name, amen.*

Listening Time

Now pray, "Holy Spirit, what are You saying to me?" Use the
space provided, or a journal or notebook, to write what He
reveals to you.

_____

_____

*The cross is the only way of salvation. And
the cross gives a new purpose to life.*
—BILLY GRAHAM

HEART SURGERY: FIND FREEDOM IN GOD'S WORD

OUR EMOTIONS CAN often lead us astray, especially when they are uncontrolled. Emotions are influenced by deep-seated beliefs, some of which may be false or rooted in painful experiences like abandonment, broken trust, or a lack of community. Today, let's explore how inviting God to search our hearts and embracing the truth in His Word can lead us to genuine freedom and transformation.

In biblical terms, the heart is the core of our being. It's where our emotions, decisions, and intellect intertwine. But as Jeremiah 17:9–10 tells us, the heart can be deceitful and beyond understanding. It's only through God's discerning eye that we can truly understand and heal our hearts. I love how *The Message* Bible puts this passage: "The heart is hopelessly dark and deceitful, a puzzle that no one can figure out. But I, GOD, search the heart and examine the mind. I get to the heart of the human. *I get to the root of things. I treat them as they really are, not as they pretend to be*" (emphasis added).

In moments of emotional turmoil it's easy to focus on the external, the outward appearance—the people, circumstances, or events that we believe are causing our distress. Yet God invites us to look deeper, to turn our attention to Him and the condition of our hearts. He wants to reveal truths to us, truths that can only be found when we surrender our pain, confusion, and misunderstandings to His care.

We need to let God expose the false belief systems that have been at work in our lives and accept the truth according to His Word. I love how Michael Dye, a certified addictions counselor, puts it in *The Genesis Process*. As the following chart shows, he encourages us to take a look at true beliefs and false beliefs and ask ourselves, "Where am I?"[1]

DIFFERENCES BETWEEN TRUE AND FALSE BELIEFS[2]

True Beliefs...	False Beliefs...
are based on the Word of God: truth and reality.	are based on fear or arise out of loss or pain.
increase the value and growth of an individual.	demean and diminish the value and growth of an individual.
are proven true through life experiences that edify both self and others.	are proven false by destructive, defensive behaviors and painful relationships.
result in safe, healthy relationships.	result in separation and isolation from others.
create peace and confidence.	create anxiety and exhaustion.
result in true emotions.	result in false emotions.

Let me show you how this works. When you go to the doctor, the first thing she asks you is, "What's wrong?" You say, "My head hurts." Then she says, "Have you been taking something?" You say, "I took some pain meds, but it just keeps hurting." She might ask how long your head has been hurting or if you have been outside. What she is trying to do is find out whether the issue is surface level or deeper.

The next thing the doctor may do is take an X-ray to see what's going on inside. Let's say she finds a tumor. She'll say, "Well, we found a mass, and that is what's causing you to feel this way and possibly affecting the way you act. But we have good news. We can go in and remove it, and everything will be great."

God is saying the same thing. The results we see on the outside reflect what we have going on inside. The Holy Spirit is the X-ray, and God is the Great Physician. He knows exactly what we must do to experience change.

Following are steps we must take to "get to the root of things" and let God heal us.

1. Let God diagnose your heart. Reflect on what emotions currently dominate your life. Are they leading you toward or away from God? Have you noticed any patterns or triggers? Ask the Lord to reveal the root causes of these emotions and what lies beneath them.

2. Accept God's truth. Look up the truths in God's Word that directly confront the falsehoods in your heart. How can these truths reshape your understanding and response to emotional challenges?

3. Shift your focus to God. How can redirecting your focus from your circumstances to God change your perspective? What might God be teaching you in this season?

4. Change beyond the surface. Behavior modification without heart transformation leads only to temporary change. How can you pursue deeper, heart-level change with God's help? If you want to change what you do, you must first change how you think about what you do. A heart transplant comes only through spending time with Jesus.

Allow God to be the Great Physician. He will give you a heart diagnosis. If you accept what He says, He will do a procedure called a John 3:16 and give you a new heart. Then He will prescribe a healthy heavenly diet plan so you can take care of that heart. Proverbs 4:23 says, "Above all else, guard your heart, for everything you do flows from it." You can't go back to the way you used to live. If you want to change destructive behaviors and emotions, you must allow God to change your *heart*.

SPIRITUAL FREEDOM STUDY

Consider the following passage.

> Search me, God, and know my heart; test me and know my anxious thoughts. See if there is any offensive way in me, and lead me in the way everlasting.
>
> —PSALM 139:23–24

Do as David did and ask God to examine your heart. Meditate on scriptures that address the emotional and spiritual needs God shows you. Journal to track your emotions and triggers, as well as the insights you gain through prayer and Scripture. Write your thoughts, feelings, and any revelations you believe God is showing you. Share your struggles with a trusted Christian friend or mentor and seek godly counsel.

_____

_____

Questions for Reflection

What you see in your life—your actions and their outcomes—are a direct result of what is happening in your heart. Are there things you repeatedly do that you don't want to do? Is your life bearing the good fruit of God's kingdom? Using the fruit of your life as a gauge, rank the condition of your heart on a scale of 1 (being the lowest) to 10 (being the highest). If you ranked yourself at an 8 or below, I challenge you to ask God to do a supernatural surgery on you. Get your pastor, elders, or a trusted friend to pray with you as you pursue a path of forgiveness and heart transformation through Christ.

_____

_____

Prayer Time (Talk to Him)

Heavenly Father, I invite Your searching gaze into the deepest parts of my heart. Expose any false beliefs and heal the wounds that cause emotional trauma.

Help me to focus on You and Your truth, knowing that only in Your Word can I find the path to true freedom. Guide me in Your everlasting ways and transform my heart to reflect Your love and wisdom. In Jesus' name, amen.

Listening Time

Now pray, "Holy Spirit, what are You saying to me?" Use the space provided, or a journal or notebook, to write what He reveals to you.

_____

_____

God never uses a person greatly
until He tests them deeply.
—A. W. TOZER

Day 4

THE TRUTH SETS US FREE

A T ITS CORE, Christianity is knowing God personally through Jesus Christ. You cannot be a Christian without knowing Jesus, no matter how often you attend church, fast, pray, or read your Bible. If you are doing these things to check a box, then you're missing the point!

Jesus described the problem this way: "These people honor me with their lips, but their hearts are far from me" (Matt. 15:8–9). You can know *about* a person without knowing that individual personally. For example, I know several actors through their movies, but I don't know them personally. I may follow them on social media and know how many kids they have or their favorite foods, but I've never met or spent time with them.

The same thing can happen in our relationship with God. We can know all about Him, but unless we have entered into a personal relationship with Jesus, we won't know Him personally. It's hard to love someone you don't know! And knowing Jesus will take a lifetime.

There are people who are hungry for freedom, but they don't want to grow in the truth. Jesus said in John 8:31–32, "If you continue in my word, you really are my disciples. You will know the truth, and the truth will set you free" (csb).

Notice that it's possible to believe in Jesus but not continue in His Word and, therefore, not be a true disciple. If you want to "know the truth," you must first understand the power of the Word of God.

I love what Tony Evans, pastor of Oak Cliff Bible Fellowship, says about the truth:

> Note two things. First, there is such a thing as truth. Truth is the absolute standard by which reality is measured. We live in a relativistic society that denies absolute truth, claiming, "What's true for you may not be true for me." But truth is not based on our feelings, experiences, or desires. Truth is God's viewpoint on every matter, and it is not subject to redefinition.
>
> Pilate would ask, "What is the truth?" (John 18:38), and the answer to that question is "Jesus." [See John 14:6, "I am the way and the truth and the life."]
>
> Second, knowing the truth results in genuine freedom. Truth alone doesn't liberate; rather, the knowledge of the truth liberates. Deliverance comes when we know the truth—that is, when we hang out in what God says.[1]

Let me explain it this way: a man has the seed; a woman has the womb. (I hope you already know this, but in today's society, you never know.) When the womb receives the seed, *boom*—a baby is produced. God's Word is the seed, we are the womb, and when we become one with the seed, *boom*—heaven on earth!

Remember when Mary, the mother of Jesus, asked the angel how she could conceive a child since she had not known a man (Luke 1:34)? The word *know* used in that verse is the same word used in John 8:32, "You will know the truth, and the truth will set you free." How can you produce heaven if you don't know God?

One of the main reasons people end up in bondage is ignorance. Isaiah 5:13 says, "My people have gone into captivity, because they have no knowledge" (NKJV). There's power in the Word of God. We need to grow in the truth because it will set us free. As we draw near to the truth through the Word of God, repent of our sin and wrong thinking, and come into agreement with what God says, we will experience the freedom He has always wanted us to have.

When you make it your ambition to know Christ, making Him known to others will be a natural result. Your passion for Jesus, born out of your relationship with Him, will influence others.

SPIRITUAL FREEDOM STUDY

Memorize John 8:31–32 in your favorite Bible translation. I'm including it here in the New International Version:

> To the Jews who had believed him, Jesus said, "If you hold to my teaching, you are really my disciples. Then you will know the truth, and the truth will set you free."

In your prayer time, write ways to apply that verse to your life.

_____

_____

Question for Reflection

Is there an area where you say you know the truth but aren't experiencing freedom? List that area (or areas) and then write what God's Word says about that subject.

_____

_____

Prayer Time (Talk to Him)

> *Heavenly Father, reveal Your truth in my life. My heart is postured in a place of humility to receive Your truth that sets hearts free. Guide me. Let Your light shine in the areas that need clarity. In Jesus' name, amen.*

Listening Time

Now pray, "Holy Spirit, what are You saying to me?" Use the space provided, or a journal or notebook, to write what He reveals to you.

_____

_____

There are two answers to every
question: God's answer and everybody
else's. And everybody else is wrong.
—Tony Evans

THE CARPENTER'S TOOLS: EMBRACE GOD'S VISION

I RECENTLY GOT PROGRESSIVE lenses. It took me five days to get acclimated to the prescription. While wearing the glasses, I felt like I was drunk because they made me so dizzy. When I alerted my doctor to the symptoms, he responded, "It'll go away in a few days. It could take a week, but if you commit to the process, eventually your eyes will acclimate to the new."

I told the doctor I would try them, but if I didn't see results soon I would return for an adjustment. The first day was the hardest. But after four days I saw way better than before—which was the whole point of getting the progressive lenses. My vision got better over time.

The same thing happened in my Christian walk. When I first got saved, I had to learn everything about who I was in Christ. I had to learn how to do life all over again. I was born again, and everything was new. So I had to adjust my vision and focus on what God was teaching me. The process was not easy, but it was so worth it.

In a similar way, God wants to give you a new perspective. New vision is often uncomfortable. Sometimes you'll feel like life is falling apart, but it's actually coming together. In these moments of discomfort we must not grab our "old glasses." Jesus wants us to embrace the new perspective—His perspective. If we don't commit to the process and stop putting on our old things, our spiritual eyes will never acclimate to what heaven is revealing.

I thank God that He encouraged me to keep my "progressive" lenses on. I thank God that He helped me endure the steps to change. Though initially my vision was blurry, I submitted to the comforting voice that told me, "You're going to be fine."

"There is a way that seems right to a man, but its end is the way of death" (Prov. 14:12, NKJV). We think we are right all the time. It's funny because when I go into prisons I always tell the guys, "Your best plan—your A-plus game—got you in prison. That day or night, you thought you had the greatest idea of all time, but it came from the devil himself."

For you, the consequences may not be as severe as getting locked up, but we all make choices based on what we think is right and how we see. We may think we know best, but it's only through God's guidance that we find the true path.

God created each of us for a unique, specific purpose. But only when we put our lives in the Master's hands can we truly use what God has given us correctly. If we don't submit our gifts to God, the enemy will pervert them for his use.

There's an old story about a creative workshop led by carpenter's tools. Brother Hammer presided over the gathering, and several people complained that he was too noisy. Brother Hammer told the crowd, "If I have to leave, Brother Screw has to leave too. You have to turn him around and around to get him to do anything." Brother Screw then pointed at Sister Sandpaper, saying, "She's rougher than I am." And so went the complaints until the carpenter of Nazareth walked in to start

His day's work. He employed every tool, each with its unique capability, to create a masterpiece.

This story reminds me of how we often view our spiritual journey. When I first started walking with Christ, I felt out of place in church. But just as a skilled carpenter knows the value of each tool in his tool kit, God showed me that my unique perspective, honed by my experiences, was valuable in His grand design.

You too must value your uniqueness. Like the carpenter's tools, we each have a role in God's plan. Our unique experiences and perspectives, even those that seem flawed or "rough," are essential in the hands of the Master Carpenter.

Over time God adjusts our spiritual vision. When we come to Christ, we begin to see our strengths and weaknesses as parts of a greater purpose. The "blurry vision" of our new faith gradually clears as we learn to trust in God's plan.

There is a story in Mark's Gospel about a blind man whom Jesus healed, and I believe his healing parallels our own spiritual awakening.

> Then they came to Bethsaida; and some people brought a blind man to Jesus and begged Him to touch him. Taking the blind man by the hand, He led him out of the village; and after spitting on his eyes and laying His hands on him, He asked him, "Do you see anything?" And he looked up and said, "I see people, but [they look] like trees, walking around." Then again Jesus laid His hands on his eyes; and the man stared intently and [his

sight] was [completely] restored, and he began to
see everything clearly.

—MARK 8:22–25, AMP

In this account there are several important truths we need
to apply to our lives:

We must seek community support. Just as the blind man
was led to Jesus, we often find our way to Christ through the
guidance of others, each person playing a unique role in our
spiritual journey.

We must step out in faith. Jesus led the man out of his
village to heal him. Similarly, God often calls us out of our
comfort zones, using our unique traits to fulfill His purpose.

We must realize our spiritual growth is often progressive.
The man's healing was gradual, which reflects our own journey
of faith. Like adjusting to a new pair of glasses, our spiritual
understanding develops over time.

When feeling uncertain about your spiritual journey,
remember the carpenter's tools. Each had a purpose, as do you.
Embrace the changes in your spiritual vision, trusting that God
is molding you into His masterpiece.

SPIRITUAL FREEDOM STUDY

Proverbs 14:12 reminds us that our ways, which often seem
right, can lead to destruction. It's only through embracing
God's perspective and teachings, and moving away from our
habitual ways of thinking and reacting, that we experience His
extraordinary works.

When you face spiritual challenges, remember that is part of the process. Stay committed to God's perspective. Commit to the process. Reflect on areas where you might still be clinging to "old glasses"—the old ways of thinking or seeing the world. Ask God to help you see these areas through His lens. Celebrate the growth and clarity you've gained.

My mentor, David Vestal, always says this to me: "Healthy things *grow*, growing things change, change brings challenges, and challenges give us an opportunity to trust in God." Don't look at your challenges as problems; see them as signs that you are growing in Christ.

Questions for Reflection

What are some "old glasses"—the familiar but limiting beliefs or perspectives—that you might still be holding on to in your spiritual life? How can you courageously embrace the new, clearer vision God is offering you?

_____

_____

Prayer Time (Talk to Him)

Heavenly Father, thank You for the new vision You provide through faith in You. Help me to navigate the discomfort that comes with spiritual growth. Teach me to see the world through Your eyes and to trust the clarity that comes from Your perspective. Guide me away from my old ways and toward Your path of truth and life. In Jesus' name, amen.

Listening Time

Now pray, "Holy Spirit, what are You saying to me?" Use the space provided, or a journal or notebook, to write what He reveals to you.

_____

_____

God does not give us everything we want, but
He does fulfill His promises, leading us along
the best and straightest paths to Himself.
—DIETRICH BONHOEFFER

TRUE REPENTANCE REQUIRES A CHANGE OF MIND

O N MAY 7, 2019, while driving near Interstate 285 in Clayton County, Georgia, Hannah Payne reportedly saw Kenneth Herring hit a semi-truck and then allegedly flee the scene. Witnessing an accident might rattle anyone, but it's what Payne did next that caused her to make national news.

Police said the then-twenty-one-year-old followed Herring and confronted him, insisting that he return to the crash site. Though she called 911 to report the accident, she ultimately shot and killed Herring, claiming he started attacking her.

Four years later, in December 2023, Payne was convicted of felony murder among other charges and sentenced to life in prison with the possibility of parole. She also will consecutively serve eight years for false imprisonment and five for possession of a firearm during the commission of a felony.[1]

I probably don't have to tell you that people are divided on whether Payne's sentence was too harsh or too lenient. But I am not sharing her story to comment on the verdict; I want to focus on her actions.

During the trial, Payne often seemed unremorseful and stared blankly through most of the proceedings. She showed the most emotion when the jury foreperson was reading the verdict that she had been found guilty on all counts. Only then did her countenance begin to shift, and she broke down more and more each time she heard the word *guilty*.

As horrible as this entire incident is, I cannot help but wonder what Payne's fate would have been if she had just repented. What if she had pleaded guilty and said she was sorry for her actions against this man and his family? Unfortunately we will never know, but we can learn a lesson from this tragic incident.

Throughout his ministry the apostle Paul had a simple message: "that they should repent and turn to God, and do works worthy of repentance" (Acts 26:20, CSB). *Repentance is a change of mind.* This brings me to a crucial truth that I want to be our focus today: to break free from sin, we must first break free from the lies we believe about it.

Consider a specific sin you struggle with. Think about what lies or misconceptions you might be holding on to about this sin. Now reflect on how this contrasts with what God's Word has revealed about that behavior.

When David was confronted by Nathan about his sin with Bathsheba, he wasted no time getting right with God. He prayed, "Create in me a pure heart, O God, and renew a steadfast spirit within me" (Ps. 51:10). Perhaps David's willingness to repent and align his thinking with God's view of the situation is why he was called a man after God's own heart even after he committed adultery and had Bathsheba's husband killed.

The Word of God teaches us, "The one who conceals his sins will not prosper, but whoever confesses and renounces them will find mercy" (Prov. 28:13, CSB). Sincere believers will continually repent until their dying day. But I believe most of us are not truly repenting.

True repentance is when we confess our sin to God and agree with what He thinks about the act. We change our minds and decide not to commit that sin again. If you apologize but repeat the same behavior, trouble will continue to plague you. As a matter of fact, saying you're sorry without changing your behavior is manipulation.

But changing your behavior is not enough. *Metanoia*, the Greek word translated "repent," refers to a change of mind.[2] Repentance is not merely about changing our actions but about aligning our thoughts with God's perspective on our sins. Are there areas in your life where you're trying to change behaviors without first changing your mindset? If so, seek God's insight to transform your thinking.

Romans 12:2 says, "Do not conform to the pattern of this world, but be transformed by the renewing of your mind. Then you will be able to test and approve what God's will is—his good, pleasing and perfect will." I want you to focus on the phrase "be transformed by the renewing of your mind." Scripture tells us that our inward and outward lives can be completely different if we are willing to go through the process of changing how we think and what we think about.

We have to think about what we're thinking about. I cannot stress that enough. You transform your life by renewing your mind. You renew your mind by thinking about what you're thinking about.

There's a difference between feeling guilty about sin and truly repenting of it. True repentance goes beyond feelings of shame; again, it's a shift in how we think about the sin. When you've done something wrong, do you repent just to escape the guilt and consequences of sin, or are you striving for true change? Spend time in prayer seeking God's help to achieve a genuine change of mind.

SPIRITUAL FREEDOM STUDY

Read 2 Timothy 2:25–26:

> Opponents must be gently instructed, in the hope that God will grant them repentance leading them to a knowledge of the truth, and that they will come to their senses and escape from the trap of the devil, who has taken them captive to do his will.

Now turn that passage into a prayer: "Lord, help me to come to my senses and escape the trap of the devil, who has taken me captive to do his will. Lead me in Your truth and liberate me from the deceptions of sin."

Questions for Reflection

In what ways might your current understanding of repentance be more about avoiding guilt or consequences than truly aligning your thoughts and actions with God's truth?

_____

_____

Consider a specific sin you struggle with. What lies or misconceptions might you be holding on to about that sin? What does God's Word say about the act or behavior? How does your thinking about it compare to what the Bible has revealed about that sin?

_____

_____

Prayer Time (Talk to Him)

> *Heavenly Father, I ask for Your guidance in my journey from deception to truth. Help me to embrace genuine metanoia, to not just feel sorry for my sins but to radically change my mindset about them. Grant me the wisdom to discern Your truth and the strength to live it out. In Jesus' name, amen.*

Listening Time

Now pray, "Holy Spirit, what are You saying to me?" Use the space provided, or a journal or notebook, to write what He reveals to you.

_____

_____

This is a work which must occur at the hour of new birth: and it does happen then in the form of repentance. The original definition of repentance is none else than "a change of mind."
—WATCHMAN NEE

Day 7

FREEDOM'S WAKE-UP CALL: REVIVAL THROUGH RIGHT PRIORITIES

I'M NOT SURE about you, but in every season of my Christian walk I have had to be reminded of my priorities. It usually happens gradually with just a slight shift here or there, but over time it's easy to get busy and start spending less time in prayer and Bible study. We can all but stop doing what we should be doing. I for one have been guilty of losing focus and running around thinking about myself.

Today, I want us to reflect on the significance of setting priorities in our spiritual journey. Just as an alarm clock's purpose is to wake us up, sometimes God sends spiritual alarms to awaken us to His presence and purpose. These alarms, often in the form of challenges or divine messages, are calls to reevaluate our priorities and align them with God's will.

Let's look at Haggai 1:2–11 (CSB):

> "The LORD of Armies says this: These people say:
> The time has not come for the house of the LORD
> to be rebuilt."
>
> The word of the LORD came through the

43

prophet Haggai: "Is it a time for you yourselves to live in your paneled houses, while this house lies in ruins?" Now, the LORD of Armies says this: "Think carefully about your ways: You have planted much but harvested little. You eat but never have enough to be satisfied. You drink but never have enough to be happy. You put on clothes but never have enough to get warm. The wage earner puts his wages into a bag with a hole in it."

The LORD of Armies says this: "Think carefully about your ways. Go up into the hills, bring down lumber, and build the house; and I will be pleased with it and be glorified," says the LORD. "You expected much, but then it amounted to little. When you brought the harvest to your house, I ruined it. Why?"

This is the declaration of the LORD of Armies. "Because my house still lies in ruins, while each of you is busy with his own house. So on your account, the skies have withheld the dew and the land its crops. I have summoned a drought on the fields and the hills, on the grain, new wine, fresh oil, and whatever the ground yields, on people and animals, and on all that your hands produce."

God wanted His temple rebuilt, but the people had excuses. As one Bible commentary puts it: "The land was still desolate after 70 years of neglect. The work was hard. They didn't have a lot of money…or manpower."[1] Doesn't that sound a lot like us? We make a bunch of excuses as to why we don't have time to do things for God, but we can always do things for ourselves. We don't have a time problem; we have a priority problem. We are more than willing to make time for the things we care about the most.

The prophet said, "Consider your ways" (Hag. 1:5, NKJV). This phrase is a Hebrew figure of speech that literally means, "Put your heart on your roads."[2] Haggai asked God's people to consider what direction their lives were heading and if they really wanted to continue that way.

I encourage you to take a moment to reflect on the same question. The Israelites needed to shift their focus from their own comfort to obeying God's word and rebuilding His house. In your life, what priorities do you need to reposition? Are there areas of your life where God is asking for more attention or more dedication?

Remember, it's not about moving God to our priority list; it's about moving ourselves to align with His eternal plan. Is your relationship with God, your spouse, or your family out of alignment? For your life to function properly, you must prioritize the important things, which are the eternal. If you get those critical relationships right, you will see significant improvement in every area of your life.

In Haggai 1 we see that God's people prioritized building their homes while God's temple remained in ruins. The people were admonished to consider, or "think carefully" about, their ways. I believe we need to do the same—to assess and execute our priorities accurately.

Our spiritual freedom journey will be marked by moments of awakening when God calls us to reassess and reposition our lives according to His will. Let's respond to these divine alarms not with reluctance but with hearts open to transformation and renewal. In doing so, we welcome a revival to our spirit that draws us ever closer to God's heart.

In the quiet moments of reflection, God whispers a wake-up call to our souls, urging us to break free from the shackles of our routines and embrace the freedom found in His purposes.

In the symphony of our lives, the call of God often arrives as a resounding alarm, urging us to awaken from complacency and step into the freedom of His divine purpose. This awakening isn't just about altering our routines or habits; it's a profound shift toward spiritual renewal and freedom. As we heed this call, we liberate ourselves from the constraints of worldly priorities and find true satisfaction and purpose in aligning with God's will. Let's embrace this journey not as a burden but as a path to spiritual freedom, where every step brings us closer to the heart of our heavenly Father.

SPIRITUAL FREEDOM STUDY

Reflect on the following verses:

> But seek first the kingdom of God and His righteousness, and all these things shall be added to you.
>
> —MATTHEW 6:33, NKJV

For where your treasure is, there your heart will be also.

—LUKE 12:34

If you love me, keep my commands.

—JOHN 14:15

Think about how you spend most of your time, talents, and financial resources. What does this tell you about where your "treasure" lies?

_____

_____

Question for Reflection

What "spiritual alarms" are going off in your life right now, and how are you responding to them? Are you ready to reposition your priorities so you can experience a deeper relationship with God?

_____

_____

Prayer Time (Talk to Him)

Heavenly Father, I ask for the courage to repent, change my mindset, and embrace Your ways. Revive

*my spirit, Lord, and renew my passion for You. In
Jesus' name, amen.*

Listening Time

Now pray, "Holy Spirit, what are You saying to me?" Use the
space provided, or a journal or notebook, to write what He
reveals to you.

_____

_____

*As long as we are content to live
without revival, we will.*
—Leonard Ravenhill

Day 8

YIELD TO GOD'S SHAKING AND TRUST HIS PERFECT TIMING

AFTER THE WAKE-UP call in Haggai chapter 1, there was a shake-up call. It's amazing that when we get saved, we think everything is instantly going to be easy and great. Well, that's not the case. Often it seems like life becomes really hard and *so* different. It's like your whole world gets turned upside down. But hold on because it's super worth it! I can testify to that. God has the perfect plan for you.

Take a moment to read Haggai 2:5–7 (csb):

> "This is the promise I made to you when you came out of Egypt, and my Spirit is present among you; don't be afraid."
>
> For the Lord of Armies says this: "Once more, in a little while, I am going to shake the heavens and the earth, the sea and the dry land. I will shake all the nations so that the treasures of all the nations will come, and I will fill this house with glory," says the Lord of Armies.

Today we will explore the profound truth that God's disruptions in our lives are often His instruments for bringing significant change and growth. Drawing from Haggai 2:5–7 we are reminded of the Lord's sovereign control over the shaking of our circumstances and His promise to be with us through it all.

I want you to understand God's shaking. I know it seems crazy, but God's kingdom is an upside-down kingdom. The Lord speaks of shaking the heavens and the earth, a metaphor for significant change and upheaval. Consider the areas in your life that you believe God is shaking. Rather than resisting or fearing these changes, ask the Lord to reveal His purpose and plan in them. Trust that He is working to bring something new and glorious out of the disruption.

Ponder the truth that God's timing is perfect, even when it doesn't align with our expectations. Just like the ancient Israelites needed to trust God's timing for their deliverance and blessing, we too are called to trust that God's plans are unfolding at the right time. When you feel impatient or anxious about the pace of change in your life, remind yourself of God's faithfulness in the past and His promises for the future.

When I got out of prison, the first nine months were crazy. I couldn't find a job. I went back to school at forty years old, but nothing made sense. So I just trusted God's leading. That season beat up on my flesh, especially my pride, but again I say God's plan is perfect.

Spend some time today reflecting on how God uses earthly events to draw our attention to spiritual and eternal realities. The story of Rahab reminds us that faith in God can transform even the most unlikely situations and people. Consider how God might be using your current circumstances to deepen your understanding of His eternal perspective and purpose for your life.

I love this illustration from Tony Evans about the power of vision and our need to have an eternal perspective:

> Have you ever been shaken up by the death of a loved one? Often, when we attend a funeral for a loved one, we start to think of things a little differently. We reflect on things that are spiritual and eternal, and they seem much closer and more real all of a sudden. When death or some other disruption occurs, the temporal life and the eternal life collide and cause us to think of what really matters. Death often forces us to see the unseen. Even in the normal times of life, God does not want us to forget to look at things from the eternal perspective.[1]

In God's divine economy, nothing is wasted—not even the shaking of our world. Each disruption, each change, is an opportunity for us to grow in faith and draw closer to God. As we embrace His perfect timing and trust in His eternal perspective, we can find peace and purpose amid the shaking.

SPIRITUAL FREEDOM STUDY

Read Haggai chapters 1 and 2, paying special attention to the following passage.

For the LORD of Armies says this: "Once more, in a little while, I am going to shake the heavens and the earth, the sea and the dry land. I will shake all the nations so that the treasures of all the nations will come, and I will fill this house with glory," says the LORD of Armies. "...The final glory of this house will be greater than the first," says the LORD of Armies.

—HAGGAI 2:6–7, 9, CSB

During your day, consider how disruptions and difficulties can be part of God's plan for your growth. The Israelites faced challenges and changes, yet these were opportunities for them to turn back to God and rebuild what was important. How can you use your current challenges as opportunities to rebuild and refocus your life according to God's plan?

_____

_____

Question for Reflection

Reflect on a recent "shaking" in your life—a disruption or change that challenged you. How did it help you grow spiritually? What did it teach you about God's character and your relationship with Him? Write these reflections in the space provided and use them as a reminder of God's faithfulness in times of change.

_____

_____

Prayer Time (Talk to Him)

> *Heavenly Father, help me to see the divine purpose in
> the challenges I face. Guide me to use these moments
> as opportunities to rebuild my life more in line with
> Your will. In Jesus' name, amen.*

Listening Time

Now pray, "Holy Spirit, what are You saying to me?" Use the
space provided, or a journal or notebook, to write what He
reveals to you.

_____

_____

They said God's time is the best, but you
have to believe that God's plan is the best
also. Never early, never late, always on time.
—AUTHOR UNKNOWN

When we come to a place where we trust that
God's timing is perfect, we can be content
no matter where we are because we know
that God will not leave us there forever.
Maintaining a passion for the present means
embracing the light we have where we are
at this time and trusting that it is enough.
—STORMIE OMARTIAN

FAITH: THE BLUEPRINT OF OBEDIENCE AND TRUST

L ET'S BEGIN TODAY by reading some passages about faith from the Old and New Testaments.

> Now faith is the reality of what is hoped for, the proof of what is not seen. For by this our ancestors were approved. *By faith* we understand that the universe was created by the word of God, so that what is seen was made from things that are not visible.
>
> —HEBREWS 11:1–3, CSB, EMPHASIS ADDED

> And without faith living within us it would be impossible to please God. For we come to God in faith knowing that he is real and that he rewards the faith of those who passionately seek him.
>
> —HEBREWS 11:6, TPT

> *By faith*, Noah built a ship in the middle of dry land. He was warned about something he couldn't see, and acted on what he was told. The result? His family was saved. His act of faith drew a sharp

line between the evil of the unbelieving world and the rightness of the believing world. As a result, Noah became intimate with God.

—HEBREWS 11:7, MSG, EMPHASIS ADDED

Make yourself an ark of gopher wood. Make rooms in the ark, and cover it with pitch inside and outside. This is how you are to make it: The ark will be 450 feet long, 75 feet wide, and 45 feet high. You are to make a roof, finishing the sides of the ark to within eighteen inches of the roof. You are to put a door in the side of the ark. Make it with lower, middle, and upper decks.

—GENESIS 6:14–16, CSB

To have a new life, you have to do something different. This is something we must understand if we are to live by faith. Listening to God and following His plan requires us to walk things out exactly as He says. But we often struggle with this because we have a problem. Let me explain, using the story of Noah.

God told Noah to get some gopher wood, and then He said, "This is how you are to make it: The ark will be 450 feet long, 75 feet wide, and 45 feet high."

This is what we would do if we were Noah: We'd go out and see that the gopher trees have to get cut, sanded down—you get the point. It looks like a long road ahead. So we'd go talk to someone who has no spiritual fruit, and they'd tell us where we can find some plywood. It's 449 feet long and 89 inches wide—not quite 450 feet long. And it isn't gopher wood, but it's cut and ready, so we decide to go the easy route; we take the shortcut. Then when we finish building and the boat sinks, we blame everyone and everything but ourselves. Yet the truth is we did things our way, not God's way, because we were in a rush and thought maybe God was in a hurry too.

First Peter 3:20 tells us that "God waited patiently in the days of Noah while the ark was being built." We must keep in mind that God always takes us through a process to grow us into maturity, and we can't rush through it. Don't move out prematurely if you want freedom. Stop modifying His plan. God will not protect what is not built according to His blueprint.

There is a powerful connection between faith and obedience. Hebrews 11 reminds us that faith is not just belief in the unseen but also a commitment to act upon that belief. I want to encourage you to think about situations in your life as we reflect on the example of Noah, whose faith and obedience led to the salvation of his family and a profound intimacy with God.

+ Faith is more than just hoping for the best; it's believing with conviction in what we cannot see and trusting God's promises. Are there areas in your life where you need to apply this kind of faith? Are there situations in which you are being called to trust God even though the outcome is uncertain?

+ Noah built an ark in the absence of rain, a tangible act of faith in God's word. Reflect on your own life. Are there instructions from

God that you are hesitant to follow because
they don't make sense in your current context?
Think about how you can embody obedience
like Noah's, even when it defies conventional
wisdom.

+ Proverbs 24 tells us that "by wisdom a house
is built, and through understanding it is estab-
lished; through knowledge its rooms are filled
with rare and beautiful treasures" (vv. 3–4).
And Jesus said, "Everyone who hears these
words of mine and does not put them into practice is like a foolish man who built his house
on sand. The rain came down, the streams rose,
and the winds blew and beat against that house,
and it fell with a great crash" (Matt. 7:26–27).

Think about the importance of building
your life according to God's blueprint. Just as
a house must be built on a solid foundation to
withstand storms, our lives must be grounded
in God's will and wisdom. Reflect on how you
can align your plans, decisions, and actions
more closely with God's design for your life.

Faith and obedience are deeply intertwined in our Christian
journey. True faith calls us to action, even in uncertainty. By
trusting in God's promises and obeying His commands, we
open ourselves to His transformative power and the fulfillment
of His plans for us.

SPIRITUAL FREEDOM STUDY

Consider the following verses:

> Now faith is the reality of what is hoped for, the
> proof of what is not seen.
>
> —HEBREWS 11:1, CSB

> For we walk by faith, not by sight.
>
> —2 CORINTHIANS 5:7, MEV

What gives you confidence that what you believe is actually
true? Reflect on how embracing faith-driven obedience can
transform your relationship with God and impact your journey.

_____

_____

Question for Reflection

Identify one area of your life where you feel God is calling you
to step out in faith. It might be a decision, a change in direction,
or an act of obedience that seems scary. How can you start
taking tangible steps of obedience, even when the path ahead
is not fully visible or clear? Commit to taking one concrete step
forward in that area this week, trusting that God will guide and
sustain you as you act in faith.

_____

_____

Prayer Time (Talk to Him)

> *Heavenly Father, grant me the courage to obey Your commands, even when they go beyond my understanding or the norms of my environment. Like Noah, let my actions reflect my absolute trust in You. Help me to build my life on the solid foundation of Your Word and Your will. Guide me in making decisions that align with Your plans and purpose for me. In Jesus' name, amen.*

Listening Time

Now pray, "Holy Spirit, what are You saying to me?" Use the space provided, or a journal or notebook, to write what He reveals to you.

_____

_____

*Faith never knows where it is being led, but
it loves and knows the One who is leading.*
—OSWALD CHAMBERS

*A revival is nothing else than a new
beginning of obedience to God.*
—CHARLES FINNEY

Day 10

TO LOVE OR NOT LOVE

I DON'T KNOW ABOUT you, but I get highly annoyed with those ancient church leaders who were always messing with Jesus. This passage from Matthew's Gospel is a case in point:

> When the Pharisees heard how he had bested the Sadducees, they gathered their forces for an assault. One of their religion scholars spoke for them, posing a question they hoped would show him up: "Teacher, which command in God's Law is the most important?"
>
> Jesus said, "'Love the Lord your God with all your passion and prayer and intelligence.' This is the most important, the first on any list. But there is a second to set alongside it: 'Love others as well as you love yourself.' These two commands are pegs; everything in God's Law and the Prophets hangs from them."
>
> —MATTHEW 22:34–40, MSG

First, the only people in the Bible trying to play fast and loose with the concept of love were the Pharisees and Sadducees. These were the super-spiritual religious leaders who cared more about titles and positions than actually doing kingdom work and spreading the gospel. Unfortunately there are people like the Pharisees and Sadducees still today. They sing and shout in church on Sunday, but they are ready to curse you out on Monday morning. But that is a discussion for another book.

Throughout the Gospels we see that the religious leaders were always trying to trip Jesus up. Yet He stayed ready for them. He was always on his p's and q's. In Matthew 22 Jesus explained that the first thing everyone needed to do was to love God. The religious leaders were probably happy to hear that because an invisible God is always easier to love than visible people. Yet I am pretty sure the second part of Jesus' response messed them up completely: He told them they had to love their neighbors as they loved themselves. *Wow!*

I am reasonably sure that word was challenging for the religious leaders because Jesus had answered them in front of witnesses. So I imagine that at the next barbecue or meet-and-greet in the fellowship hall, when the religious elite were trying to make their plates first without regard for anyone else, someone spoke up and said, "Hey, Pharisee, my man. Remember that Jesus said you have to love me like yourself. So why are you trying to give me that burnt-to-a-crisp hot dog?" There may not be a biblical record of this question, but I believe someone called these leaders out sooner or later.

To be sure the Pharisees got the message, Jesus described the commandments to love the Lord with all your passion and to love your neighbor as yourself as the pegs on which every other commandment hangs. So what exactly is love?

Love is patient and kind; it is not jealous or conceited or proud; love is not ill-mannered or selfish or irritable; love does not keep a record of wrongs; love is not happy with evil, but is happy with the truth. Love never gives up; and its faith, hope, and patience never fail.

Love is eternal. There are inspired messages, but they are temporary; there are gifts of speaking in strange tongues, but they will cease; there is knowledge, but it will pass. For our gifts of knowledge and of inspired messages are only partial; but when what is perfect comes, then what is partial will disappear.

When I was a child, my speech, feelings, and thinking were all those of a child; now that I am an adult, I have no more use for childish ways. What we see now is like a dim image in a mirror; then we shall see face-to-face. What I know now is only partial; then it will be complete—as complete as God's knowledge of me.

Meanwhile these three remain: faith, hope, and love; and the greatest of these is love.

—1 CORINTHIANS 13:4–13, GNT

The kind of love described in this passage is summed up in the Greek word *agape*. This isn't romantic love or brotherly love. It is unconditional, sacrificial love, the kind of love God shows us and empowers us to reveal to others.

According to one commentary, "Biblical agape love is the

love of choice, the love of serving with humility, the highest
kind of love, the noblest kind of devotion, the love of the will
(intentional, a conscious choice) and not motivated by superfi-
cial appearance, emotional attraction, or sentimental relationship. Agape is not based on pleasant emotions or good feelings
that might result from a physical attraction or a familial bond.
Agape chooses as an act of self-sacrifice to serve the recipient."[1]

Love is the most excellent quality a Christian can possess, and
it is God's desire—His preferred choice—that we demonstrate
His agape love to those around us. But it will take supernatural
power to love as purely as 1 Corinthians 13 instructs. It takes
maturity to put away childish and immature affection that is
one-sided, short-sighted, and limited.

It is clear that if we plan to love the way God intends, we will
stop making comparisons, being envious, keeping track of wrongs,
and holding grudges. I heard a man who had been married for
more than forty years say a good marriage is the committed
union of two people with big hearts and short memories. I love
that! It means they love deeply and forgive daily.

If we are to honor Jesus' instruction in Matthew 22:37–39,
we must commit to loving like God loves, which also means
forgiving like God forgives.

SPIRITUAL FREEDOM STUDY

Memorize 1 John 4:7–8:

> Dear friends, let us love one another, for love
> comes from God. Everyone who loves has been
> born of God and knows God. Whoever does not
> love does not know God, because God is love.

Name a person or group of people you want to love better.

_____

_____

Now, write a prayer for this person or group of people.

_____

_____

Question for Reflection

How can you practice agape love in your daily life, especially toward those who challenge or disagree with you, and reflect Jesus' command to love our neighbors as ourselves?

_____

_____

Prayer Time (Talk to Him)

> *Heavenly Father, in moments when loving others feels beyond my reach, remind me of Your love for me. Your love is patient, kind, and never failing. Holy Spirit, empower me to forgive, to let go of grievances, and to celebrate the truth in love. May my life reflect the beauty of Your love to a world in desperate need of hope and healing.*

Grant me the spiritual freedom that comes from living out Your commandments of love, freeing me from the chains of judgment, envy, and pride. Fill me with Your Spirit, that I may be an agent of Your peace and love in every word I speak and in every action I take. In Jesus' name I pray, amen.

Listening Time

Now pray, "Holy Spirit, what are You saying to me?" Use the space provided, or a journal or notebook, to write what He reveals to you.

_____

_____

Love is the only force capable of transforming an enemy into a friend.
—Martin Luther King Jr.

PRACTICE LISTENING

THE BIBLE HAS a lot to say about the importance of listening. Take the following scriptures, for example:

> My dear brothers and sisters, take note of this: Everyone should be quick to listen, slow to speak and slow to become angry.
>
> —JAMES 1:19

> My son, pay attention to my words and be willing to learn; open your ears to my sayings. Do not let them escape from your sight; keep them in the center of your heart.
>
> —PROVERBS 4:20–21, AMP

Everyone has ears, but not everyone is willing to listen. Every day I practice listening. Because I like to talk, I sometimes have to work at it twice as hard. When I talk with my wife and kids, I listen to hear their hearts. When I pray, I pause to hear what the Holy Spirit is saying. When I read the Bible, I meditate on the passage. I don't want to just see the words on the page. I want to know the context and application.

God encourages us to learn His sayings and pay attention to His instructions. I know that is hard for some of us, especially those who like to put things together without the directions. The items usually end up wobbly with twenty screws left over when they're done! It would have been so much easier if they'd just followed the manufacturer's instructions.

Listening and obeying are two sides of a coin. Scripture tells us, "Out of the abundance of the heart the mouth speaks" (Matt. 12:34, MEV). So when God speaks, I listen to hear His heart in what He's saying. I might not be the smartest person, but I don't have to be. God has all the wisdom. When my heart is linked to His, I delight in His Word, and He will grant me the desires of my heart. (See Psalm 37:4.)

But how can we truly listen to God if we don't learn to listen in everyday situations—as we talk with our families, friends, and coworkers? And if we do not listen to God, how can we effectively lead our families and make Christ-honoring decisions? This is why learning to listen is so vital. There is an old saying that we have two ears and one mouth because we should listen twice as much as we speak. Everyone should be "slow to speak and slow to become angry" (Jas. 1:19). A hot temper doesn't produce the righteousness of God. So before we throw our tantrums, we should think twice about our responses.

Yes, tantrums are not only thrown by toddlers. People of all ages can be guilty of this behavior. But like toddlers, when adults exhibit this type of emotional response, we can be sure they are not listening!

Listening to God and making decisions based on the information He provides is vital to achieving and maintaining abundant life. And there are times when listening to the voice of the Father can mean the difference between life and death!

Let's go to the Book of Genesis and look at the account of someone who heeded God's voice and instructions:

> Now the earth was corrupt in God's sight and was full of violence. God saw how corrupt the earth had become, for all the people on earth had corrupted their ways. So God said to Noah, "I am going to put an end to all people, for the earth is filled with violence because of them. I am surely going to destroy both them and the earth. So make yourself an ark of cypress wood; make rooms in it and coat it with pitch inside and out. This is how you are to build it: The ark is to be three hundred cubits long, fifty cubits wide, and thirty cubits high. Make a roof for it, leaving below the roof an opening one cubit high all around.
>
> "Put a door in the side of the ark and make lower, middle and upper decks. I am going to bring floodwaters on the earth to destroy all life under the heavens, every creature that has the breath of life in it. Everything on earth will perish. But I will establish my covenant with you, and you will enter the ark—you and your sons and your wife and your sons' wives with you. You are to bring into the ark two of all living creatures, male and female, to keep them alive with you. Two of every kind of bird, of every kind of animal, and of every kind of creature that moves along the ground will come to you to be kept alive. You are to take every

kind of food that is to be eaten and store it away
as food for you and for them."

Noah did everything just as God commanded
him.

—Genesis 6:11–22

Whoa. Talk about having a bad day! Can you imagine God coming to you and telling you He is sorry that He created the human race? Think about that for a minute. God was not saying He was sorry for creating the family in the fourth house down the street. He wasn't even saying He was sorry for creating a specific town or city. Nope. He said, "Man, this human part of creation is not quite going how I expected. I am done with this batch, and we must start from scratch!"

It would be disturbing to hear the Creator express such shocking dissatisfaction with the human race. But then, right before a sense of panic and fear sets in, imagine God says you have found favor with Him and He is going to save you and your entire family. Yet as incredible as it may feel to be spared, there is a catch. God has chosen you for a special assignment: to build an ark that will allow Him to "restart" humanity.

Imagine if social media had been around at that time! Noah would have been "memed" into oblivion. TikTokers would have had a field day mocking him, and YouTubers would have hounded him and his family daily. The Noah family would have had no peace. And to add insult to injury, many scholars believe it had never rained before the great flood, so Noah just looked crazy.

Despite all the odds stacked against him, Noah did everything God instructed him to do. As a result, his family was saved. Noah's radical obedience is an excellent example of the benefit of listening to God even when the directions make no sense at the time.

SPIRITUAL FREEDOM STUDY

When we listen in prayer, we may not always hear an audible voice, but we encounter the presence of the Almighty. We discern His will through the gentle nudges of the Holy Spirit, the comforting reassurances of God's Word, and the peace that surpasses understanding.

Listening requires intentionality. It demands our time, our attention, and our willingness to be receptive. It asks us to lay aside our own agendas and trust that God's plan is far greater than our own.

As we commit to the practice of listening for spiritual freedom, let us remember the wisdom of Psalm 46:10: "Be still, and know that I am God."

Question for Reflection

Reflect on a time when you wish you had listened to God and your failure to or delay in doing so impacted you negatively. What are two things you learned from that situation that will help you avoid repeating that mistake?

_____

_____

Prayer Time (Talk to Him)

Heavenly Father, I come before You with a heart willing to listen. In the midst of life's noise and distractions I seek the stillness of Your presence. Help me to quiet my mind and open my ears to hear Your voice. May Your words of wisdom, comfort, and guidance become clear to me. Give me the patience to wait on You. In Jesus' name, amen.

Listening Time

Now pray, "Holy Spirit, what are You saying to me?" Use the space provided, or a journal or notebook, to write what He reveals to you.

_____

_____

God gave us two ears and one mouth, so we
ought to listen twice as much as we speak.
—UNKNOWN

Day 12

CHOOSING YOUR CREW: THE POWER OF GODLY CONNECTIONS

I WAS GOING TO title this day "You Need a Crew," but the truth is that most of us have a crew. The key is figuring out whether you are with the right crew, or if you even know how to choose.

Today we're going to look at the importance of the company we keep and the significant impact our relationships have on our life's journey. Just as Jesus carefully chose His disciples, we too are called to wisely select those with whom we walk through life.

We usually choose our friends according to their personalities and packaging—their looks, popularity, and so on. Those are never the qualities you need unless you are in organized crime and are picking a crew based on the gifts and talents they need to get a job done. Funny how the enemy perverts God's plan. We all have unique strengths and gifts, but we were designed to use them to build God's kingdom, not Satan's.

This makes me think back to when I was locked down. Not surprisingly, one of the things that comes up when you are doing time is how to pull off the ideal prison break. Several types of prisoners would usually be involved. There was always the guy with the idea or the detailed plan; this was typically the one who could access the prison blueprints or knew the architecture of the facility. Then there was the guy who served as the muscle, and another guy who could access a vehicle and would be the getaway driver. Every prison break needed a crew!

God designed you and knows what you need to get through life. He can provide the freedom you desire; He has the actual plans, the muscle, and the vehicle. In this case the vehicle I am referring to is the Holy Spirit. When we embrace the Spirit, He will always lead us where we need to go.

Think about or meditate on the biblical truth that we are created for community. God's declaration in Genesis 2:18 that "it is not good for the man to be alone" underlines our need for companionship and collaboration. Reflect on your current circle of friends and associates. Do they align with the kind of person you aspire to be? Are they helping you to grow in your faith and purpose? The Bible says, "He who walks with wise men will be wise, but the companion of fools will suffer harm" (Prov. 13:20, NASB). Are you constantly suffering harm? If your life is constantly falling apart, maybe you're surrounded by fools.

Think about the people you spend the most time with. Are they influencing you positively, leading you toward wisdom and righteousness? Consider the changes you might need to make in your relationships to ensure they are contributing positively to your spiritual growth.

When Jesus was about to select His disciples, He spent the whole night in prayer before making His decision. This teaches us the importance of seeking God's guidance in our relationships. Consider the significant relationships in your life.

Have you sought God's direction in these relationships? Ask God to help you make wise choices that reflect His will.

You will never experience freedom without community. Even if you have been hurt by people in your past, you must forgive them and move on. New experiences can help you deal with deeply rooted issues, and new people can help you heal from the pain of your past.

For example, my son, a barber now, initially struggled with his career. Though he's an excellent barber and makes great money, he was terrible when he first went to barber school. When he was presented with an opportunity to further his skills, I remember him coming to me with doubt. He said, "Dad, I'm not good at this. I'm going to quit." I told him, "Jonathan, even though I've given like five million sermons, I still don't feel I'm the greatest preacher on the planet. But while there is still much to learn, I will not give up. And you shouldn't either." And guess what? He didn't!

The same concept can be applied to many other scenarios. Without a community, often we opt out of things that we deem too difficult. You cannot have a successful life by yourself. The hand is only useful when connected to the wrist, and the wrist can only function if it is connected to the body. In fact, any body part that is disconnected and left by itself is weird. It is like Frankenstein's monster—not good!

You cannot be effective in the kingdom by yourself. Everyone needs community. The people we surround ourselves with greatly influence the direction of our lives. Like Jesus, we should be intentional in choosing our crew, seeking God's guidance and looking for relationships that sharpen and strengthen our character. Your friends are a prophecy of your future because you will likely become like them, so choose wisely.

In the garden of our lives, the people we surround ourselves with are the flowers or the weeds; they either nourish our growth or hinder it. Choose wisely, for every relationship has the power to shape not just the path you walk but the person you become.

The course of your life is not just determined by who you are; it is also impacted by your crew. Every prison break needs a crew.

Remember, you can't pick right if you see wrong. Go to the Lord in prayer and let the One who sees and knows the plan help you choose!

SPIRITUAL FREEDOM STUDY

> As iron sharpens iron, so a man sharpens the countenance of his friend.
>
> —PROVERBS 27:17, NKJV

> Do not be misled: "Bad company corrupts good character."
>
> —1 CORINTHIANS 15:33

Meditate on the previous verses. Then take some time to evaluate your current friendships and relationships. Identify those that are edifying and those that may be leading you away from God's path. Consider ways to strengthen your godly connections, and seek God's guidance for any needed changes in your relationships.

Questions for Reflection

Consider the current state of your relationships. How are they influencing your spiritual growth and alignment with God's will? Ask yourself, "Are there relationships in my life that need reevaluation or redirection under God's guidance? How can I more actively seek and cultivate godly friendships that not only support me but also challenge me to grow in my faith?"

List the names of everyone who encourages you, ignites your faith, and generally helps you see the positive in every situation.

_____

_____

_____

Now list everyone in that group who has a real, authentic relationship with Jesus.

_____

_____

_____

Now list the people you would trust with your life.

_____

_____

Prayer Time (Talk to Him)

> *Heavenly Father, give me discernment and wisdom regarding my relationships. Let my friendships and associations glorify You and lead me in the path of righteousness. In Jesus' name, amen.*

Listening Time

Now pray, "Holy Spirit, what are You saying to me?" Use the space provided, or a journal or notebook, to write what He reveals to you.

_____

_____

Show me your friends and I'll show you your future. The people you're hanging out with today are shaping the person you will become tomorrow.
—CRAIG GROESCHEL

Alone we can do so little; together we can do so much.
—HELEN KELLER

THE TRANSFORMATIVE POWER OF FORGIVENESS

Forgiveness is a cornerstone of the Christian faith. Today we're going to delve into the heart of forgiveness—an act that not only releases others but also sets us free.

Let's begin by reading what Jesus said about forgiveness in Matthew 18.

> Then Peter came to Jesus and asked, "Lord, if my brother keeps on sinning against me, how many times do I have to forgive him? Seven times?"
>
> "No, not seven times," answered Jesus, "but seventy times seven, because the Kingdom of heaven is like this. Once there was a king who decided to check on his servants' accounts. He had just begun to do so when one of them was brought in who owed him millions of dollars. The servant did not have enough to pay his debt, so the king ordered him to be sold as a slave, with his wife and his children and all that he had, in order to pay the debt. The servant fell on his knees before the king. 'Be patient with me,' he begged, 'and I will

pay you everything!' The king felt sorry for him, so he forgave him the debt and let him go.

"Then the man went out and met one of his fellow servants who owed him a few dollars. He grabbed him and started choking him. 'Pay back what you owe me!' he said. His fellow servant fell down and begged him, 'Be patient with me, and I will pay you back!' But he refused; instead, he had him thrown into jail until he should pay the debt. When the other servants saw what had happened, they were very upset and went to the king and told him everything. So he called the servant in. 'You worthless slave!' he said. 'I forgave you the whole amount you owed me, just because you asked me to. You should have had mercy on your fellow servant, just as I had mercy on you.' The king was very angry, and he sent the servant to jail to be punished until he should pay back the whole amount."

And Jesus concluded, "That is how my Father in heaven will treat every one of you unless you forgive your brother from your heart."

—Matthew 18:21–35, GNT

Man, you've got to love Peter. For those who are parents, Peter may remind you of that one kid that you love but who works you. He works your patience, your nerves, and your sanity, but you love him anyway! In this passage we see that Peter wants to know how many times he must forgive someone who has done him wrong. I am sure he was sorry he asked because Jesus gave him a math problem that racked his brain, and now Peter was accountable for the information he had been given.

Not only did Jesus give Peter an unexpectedly high number, but He also told a parable to drill in the fact that forgiveness is not optional in the kingdom of God. Biblical forgiveness is not about keeping count but about losing count. As you go about your day, think of someone you may be struggling to forgive. Consider the freedom that would come from letting go of the need for retribution or keeping score.

The passage in Matthew 18 is not the only illustration of forgiveness in Scripture. One of my favorites is the example of Joseph. Every time I read his story I admire him a little more. If you follow Joseph's life, you will see someone who mastered the art of forgiveness. I don't know if anyone would blame Joseph for holding a grudge, but time after time, no matter how bad his situation got, he always responded the right way. He never attacked his accuser. But I don't want to get ahead of myself. For those who are new to Joseph's story or need a refresher, let's review.

Joseph was the eleventh of Jacob's twelve sons. Jealous that their father favored Joseph, the brothers sold Joseph into slavery, and he ended up wrongfully imprisoned in Egypt. But because of the hand of God on his life, Joseph was eventually promoted from the prison to a seat of power, second only to Pharaoh.

It could easily be argued that Joseph's brothers set his life on a path of destruction and turned his world upside down. Yet years later when Joseph finally ran into his brothers, he did not hold a grudge against them. He comforted them and explained that their actions touched off a series of events that put Joseph in a position to save lives, including theirs and their children's. Most people would not be able to show such grace and mercy, but Joseph not only forgave his brothers; he also chose to bless them.

> And Joseph said to them, Fear not; for am I in the place of God? [Vengeance is His, not mine.] As for you, you thought evil against me, but God meant it for good, to bring about that many people should be kept alive, as they are this day. Now therefore, do not be afraid. I will provide for and support you and your little ones. And he comforted them [imparting cheer, hope, strength] and spoke to their hearts [kindly].
> —GENESIS 50:19–21, AMPC

Joseph's response reveals a powerful lesson we all need to learn: *we must forgive even those who don't necessarily deserve to be forgiven.*

The forgiveness is not for their benefit; it is for yours. I recently read a Johns Hopkins Medicine article that said "studies have found that the act of forgiveness can reap huge rewards for your health, lowering the risk of heart attack; improving cholesterol levels and sleep; and reducing pain, blood pressure, and levels of anxiety, depression and stress."[1]

Somebody is about to get healed today! You thought that bacon was driving up your blood pressure when it was really that rotten person you are still mad at from the fourth grade. I'm kidding...kind of. Some of us need to leave the bacon alone *and* forgive. I want you to eat healthy so you can live life to the fullest, but it doesn't matter how clean your diet is if you are walking around holding grudges heavy enough to bench press! Please hear me: You have to let that go, not because the person deserves it but because your future in God is greater than the weight of your past.

Forgiveness is necessary because it requires you to *release the past and focus on the future.* Some people think forgiveness means they must be friends with the person who wronged them or stay in fellowship with them. The devil is a liar! Releasing the wrong through forgiveness is a supernatural, godly activity; intentionally choosing not to be around people who hurt you emotionally, mentally, physically, or sexually is a natural act of wisdom.

You can forgive and still recognize that the person should never have access to you or anyone connected to you again. God has given you wisdom and discernment. My point is simply that to experience an abundant life, you need to release the pain of the harm you experienced in the past. Despite being severely wronged by his brothers, Joseph chose forgiveness, and he was able to see God's hand in his trials. Reflect on the times you have felt wronged or hurt. How can you shift your perspective to see God's greater plan and purpose amid those challenges?

It's also possible that you need to forgive yourself. Once you accept Christ into your life, God is no longer holding your sin against you. If He's not condemning you, you need to stop condemning yourself. Forgiveness unlocks the chains that others tried to put on you and the ones you have kept on yourself. It is time to release it all today.

I had to forgive a whole list of people. Let me tell you what made it easier. I held a grudge against my dad, and one day the Lord spoke to me and said, "He only did what he knew to do." People only do what they know to do. That's why Jesus said, "Father, forgive them, for they know not what they do" (Luke 23:34, MEV). Wow, did that bless me. My judgment went low, and grace and mercy went high. Today I live in total freedom, and you can too.

A preacher once said, "Holding an offense against someone is like being a jailer, while the offending party is in the jail. You're keeping them in there. You alone have the key to let them out, but you just won't, because of what they did to you. The problem is, since you're the jailer, you're stuck there too. Oh, the person might be behind the bars, but you can't go anywhere either. The only way to set yourself free is by letting them go, too."[2]

Will you let someone go free today? Will you turn the key? Will you forgive?

SPIRITUAL FREEDOM STUDY

Forgiveness is a powerful act that frees us from the chains of bitterness and resentment. It is not always easy, but it is always necessary for our spiritual growth and well-being. As we learn to forgive others and ourselves, we open the door to a life of freedom and abundance in Christ.

Reflect on Jesus' words in Matthew 6:14–15:

> If you forgive other people when they sin against you, your heavenly Father will also forgive you.

But if you do not forgive others their sins, your
Father will not forgive your sins.

Identify someone you need to forgive or seek forgiveness
from. Make a conscious decision to forgive or ask for forgiveness,
whether in prayer, through a conversation, or by writing a letter.
Remember, this step is more about your freedom and growth in
Christ than the response of the other person.

Today, I commit to the Lord this list of people I need to
forgive:

_____

_____

Questions for Reflection

How is holding on to unforgiveness helping you? What might
you gain if you let go of the hurt?

_____

_____

When we forgive, we are trusting God for the results, even
if we don't understand. Forgiveness must be really important
considering that Jesus said, "If you do not forgive others their
sins, your Father will not forgive your sins" (Matt. 6:15). God
doesn't want to hurt us. Trust Him and believe that forgiveness
is an invitation to the supernatural.

Prayer Time (Talk to Him)

Heavenly Father, I come before You with a heart seeking understanding and the grace to embrace forgiveness as You have taught us. Lord, as I reflect on Your Word, I am reminded of Your mercy and the transformative power of forgiveness.

I confess, Lord, that there are times when forgiving others seems beyond my reach. The pain of past wrongs can feel too heavy, the memories too sharp. Yet I know that in Your wisdom You have called us to forgive, not just for the sake of others but for the healing and freedom of our own souls.

God, give me the strength to let go of bitterness and the courage to forgive as You have forgiven me. Help me to remember that forgiveness is an act of obedience to You and a pathway to peace. In forgiving others, let me find release from the chains of resentment and step into the freedom and wholeness You offer.

Teach me, Lord, to see those who have wronged me through Your eyes of love and compassion. Fill my heart with Your grace that I may extend it to others, even when it's difficult. Guide me in the practical steps of forgiveness, whether it means reaching out, having difficult conversations, or simply letting go in prayer.

I pray also for anyone I may have wronged intentionally or unintentionally. Give me the humility to seek forgiveness and the wisdom to restore broken relationships in a manner that honors You.

Thank You, Father, for the gift of Your forgiveness that makes all of this possible. Through the power of the Holy Spirit, help me to live out the freedom that comes from forgiving and being forgiven. In Jesus' name, amen.

Listening Time

Now pray, "Holy Spirit, what are You saying to me?" Use the space provided, or a journal or notebook, to write what He reveals to you.

_____

_____

*We must develop and maintain the capacity
to forgive. He who is devoid of the power to
forgive is devoid of the power to love....There
is some good in the worst of us and some
evil in the best of us. When we discover
this, we are less prone to hate our enemies.*
—Martin Luther King Jr.

*To be a Christian means to forgive
the inexcusable, because God has
forgiven the inexcusable in you.*
—C. S. Lewis

LIFE'S THREADS: GOD'S WORK BEHIND THE SCENES

A GUY WENT TO India and encountered a man working on a tapestry. The visitor asked the craftsman, "Hey, how much for the tapestry?" And the guy gave him some crazy price, like two grand or something nuts. All the tourist could see was a jumble of colors and a few loose threads, and he thought, "Two grand for that?"

However, when the visitor walked around the tapestry to look at the other side, he saw something extraordinary. All things were working together. Every blue, yellow, and green thread had a purpose, and the image they formed was without compare. The craftsman's price didn't seem too costly once he saw the intricacy of the design.

Our lives are like that tapestry. Just as every thread has a purpose, so does every season of our lives. The Father is working everything together to mature us, just as the Word says.

> And we know that for those who love God all things work together for good, for those who are called according to his purpose.
>
> —ROMANS 8:28, ESV

> But now, O LORD, you are our Father; we are the
> clay, and you are our potter; we are all the work of
> your hand.
>
> —ISAIAH 64:8, ESV

We are on this earth to reveal God's glory! Every single strand is about Jesus living through us. Our purpose is not to achieve whatever the world says success is, so you can't look through those lenses. You can't bring that into Christianity. God works all things together for our good because we love Him and we're called according to His purpose.

When we look into the beauty of Scripture, we see the greater scheme God is fashioning. We can trust that everything works together for our good because the Bible says so. Even when you feel insecure about your life, understand that God is molding, leading, and guiding you toward something greater for His glory.

Let me paint you another picture. I recently hung out with some of my church family, and we attended a pottery class. When I asked the instructor for advice (since it was my first time), she said, "Well, you've got to take the clay and beat that sucker! You never let the clay tell you what to do." Her response made me pause for a moment. I wondered if that's how God feels!

The instructor said, "You're going to hold it firm and make sure it's still. Any sudden movements will misshape the clay."

That's when I realized the same thing happens with us. Chaos is sure to follow when we don't let God shape us and do things in our own way instead of following His blueprint. However, when we stay centered in Christ, we allow Him to move through us and make the crooked paths straight.

The pottery experience was eye-opening for me. I had done everything wrong my whole life, and now I am determined to get things right. Life is short, and I don't want to waste time. Molding pottery taught me the value of being still and waiting on God. He is our Potter. He sees the fragility of our thoughts, emotions, dreams, and desires and knows how to help us accomplish His divine will for our lives. He causes all the decisions, sidetracks, and missteps to still work for our good because we love Him and ultimately are called for His purpose.

God not only redeems time, but He restores years! I am a witness. I challenge you to release your worries about your past mistakes to Him and trust Him with your future. God will complete the good work He began in you.

SPIRITUAL FREEDOM STUDY

Memorize Jeremiah 29:11 in your favorite Bible translation. I've put my favorite translation here.

> "For I know the plans I have for you," declares the
> LORD, "plans to prosper you and not to harm you,
> plans to give you hope and a future."

In your prayer time, write how that verse applies to your life.

_____

_____

Questions for Reflection

How can you align yourself with God's will in your journey to freedom, trusting that He is orchestrating all things for your good? What steps can you take to align your choices and attitudes with His plan for your life?

_____

_____

Prayer Time (Talk to Him)

> *Heavenly Father, Your Word assures me that "all things work together for good to those who love God, to those who are called according to [Your] purpose" [Rom. 8:28, MEV]. In times of uncertainty, help me to not lean on my own understanding and to acknowledge You in all my ways so that every crooked path can be straight. May I find peace and hope in the knowledge that You are working all things together for my good and for Your glory. In Jesus' name, amen.*

Listening Time

Now pray, "Holy Spirit, what are You saying to me?" Use the space provided, or a journal or notebook, to write what He reveals to you.

_____

_____

In the tapestry of life, God is the weaver, and
every thread, even the darkest one, is an
essential part of the masterpiece He is creating.
—AUTHOR UNKNOWN

TRIALS AND TRIBULATIONS

I BELIEVE WE PASTORS sometimes do our congregants a disservice. We spend lots of time convincing people to give their lives to Christ so they can have a better life, but we don't devote enough time to explaining that even with God in our lives we will still have trouble. As a result, when trouble comes, people don't know how to engage in spiritual warfare.

Waging war in the spirit requires knowing how and when to fight. But often we don't know when to fight because we don't know the difference between a trial and a temptation. Temptation is when the enemy is soliciting you to do what he wants you to do. A trial is often a test from the Lord. However, both can happen simultaneously and sometimes go hand in hand.

When you are unaware of what a temptation is, it is easier to succumb to one. This is what happened to Eve in the Garden of Eden.

> Now the serpent was more crafty than any of the wild animals the LORD God had made. He said to the woman, "Did God really say, 'You must not eat from any tree in the garden'?"
>
> The woman said to the serpent, "We may eat

fruit from the trees in the garden, but God did say,
'You must not eat fruit from the tree that is in the
middle of the garden, and you must not touch it,
or you will die.'"

"You will not certainly die," the serpent said to
the woman. "For God knows that when you eat
from it your eyes will be opened, and you will be
like God, knowing good and evil."

When the woman saw that the fruit of the tree
was good for food and pleasing to the eye, and also
desirable for gaining wisdom, she took some and
ate it. She also gave some to her husband, who was
with her, and he ate it. Then the eyes of both of
them were opened, and they realized they were
naked; so they sewed fig leaves together and made
coverings for themselves.

—GENESIS 3:1–7

Eve was unaware the serpent was pushing her away from
God and did not have her best interest in mind. He used her
lack of wisdom to manipulate her toward his goals, which he
still does even today. The enemy will make you question the
goodness of the Lord by clouding your mind with earthly
distractions.

Most people can relate to desiring something they don't have.
When we allow that desire to take our focus off the Lord we
expose ourselves to the seven deadly sins: lust, greed, gluttony,
envy, sloth (laziness), wrath (anger), and pride. Eve had
everything she needed in the garden, but the enemy slithered in

and tempted her to seek "more," leading her to make a mistake that caused her perfect life with Adam to unravel.

Before we judge Eve too harshly, consider that social media is a modern-day enemy that opens us up to those same deadly sins. I can't tell you how many couples I counsel who have completely unrealistic goals for their relationship based on something they saw on Facebook or Instagram. "#CoupleGoals" has people lusting, envying, and walking in pride instead of living as God intended with the person they committed to be with for life.

The serpent's words and actions in Genesis 3 teach us a lot about temptation. He said, "For God knows that when you eat from it your eyes will be opened, and you will be like God, knowing good and evil" (v. 5). That statement was only effective because Eve was willing to question the goodness of the Lord and His ability to satisfy her desires. The enemy used Eve's greed against her.

Notice that in verse 6, "when the woman saw that the fruit of the tree was good for food and pleasing to the eye, and also desirable for gaining wisdom, she took some and ate it." When she saw it as pleasing to her eyes and flesh, the Lord's admonishment went out the window! Before the fruit even touched her lips, Eve had questioned and overruled God's instructions.

Temptation begins in your mind as you question the intentionality of God. You think, "If God cared, why would He let me go through this?" "Why do bad things happen to good people?" "How can this be God?"

As I said, temptations and trials often overlap. But the critical thing to understand about trials—bad things happening to good people—is that they are a component of the Christian life. God often sends trials to teach you something you'll need later in your life. Before David faced Goliath, he had overcome the trials of defeating a lion and a bear.

In the first chapter of James we are instructed to count it all joy when we experience trials, because the testing of our faith produces perseverance. The Amplified Bible breaks it down this way:

> Consider it nothing but joy, my brothers and sisters, whenever you fall into various trials. Be assured that the testing of your faith [through experience] produces endurance [leading to spiritual maturity and inner peace]. And let endurance have its perfect result and do a thorough work, so that you may be perfect and completely developed [in your faith], lacking in nothing.
>
> —JAMES 1:2–4, AMP

There are some trials God allows in our lives to help us build endurance, perseverance, and patience. The key is to go through them with grace and integrity so you can gain everything God intended for you. The worst thing in life is getting only some of what you were supposed to have.

Think about a fast-food combo. Have you ever had something left out of your bag? Whether the missing item was silverware, a sauce packet, or a part of the meal (like your fries), you are annoyed and ready to speak to the manager! Well, when it comes to trials, God is the general manager, and He ensures that everything required for your order is in your bag.

The key is avoiding giving in to temptation while you are going through the trial. It can be tempting to cheat when your spouse is not fulfilling your needs, but it is better to seek God and good counsel. It can be tempting to medicate the pain of life with drugs, alcohol, or even food, but it is better to fellowship with like-minded believers and do life with them. You will often discover that someone else has survived what you are going through right now!

SPIRITUAL FREEDOM STUDY

If you want to master trials and temptations, I suggest you read all forty-two chapters of Job. Because I know you may be pressed for time, I have given you two primary passages to study. You can view them as bookends: how Job's journey started and how it ended.

> And the LORD said to Satan, "Have you considered my servant Job, that there is none like him on the earth, a blameless and upright man, who fears God and turns away from evil?" Then Satan answered the LORD and said, "Does Job fear God for no reason? Have you not put a hedge around him and his house and all that he has, on every side? You have blessed the work of his hands, and his possessions have increased in the land. But stretch out your hand and touch all that he has, and he will curse you to your face." And the LORD said to Satan, "Behold, all that he has is in your hand. Only against him do not stretch out your

hand." So Satan went out from the presence of the
Lord.

—JOB 1:8–12, ESV

And the LORD restored the fortunes of Job, when
he had prayed for his friends. And the LORD gave
Job twice as much as he had before. Then came
to him all his brothers and sisters and all who
had known him before, and ate bread with him
in his house. And they showed him sympathy and
comforted him for all the evil that the LORD had
brought upon him. And each of them gave him a
piece of money and a ring of gold.

And the LORD blessed the latter days of Job
more than his beginning. And he had 14,000
sheep, 6,000 camels, 1,000 yoke of oxen, and
1,000 female donkeys. He had also seven sons
and three daughters. And he called the name
of the first daughter Jemimah, and the name of
the second Keziah, and the name of the third
Keren-happuch. And in all the land there were
no women so beautiful as Job's daughters. And
their father gave them an inheritance among their
brothers. And after this Job lived 140 years, and
saw his sons, and his sons' sons, four generations.
And Job died, an old man, and full of days.

—JOB 42:10–17, ESV

Question for Reflection

Job's story begins with God not only allowing Satan to test him but also offering Job up for the test. What revelations do you see about the differences between trials and temptations as you read Job's story?

_____

_____

Prayer Time (Talk to Him)

> *Havenly Father, in the midst of trials and tribulations I turn to You for comfort and guidance. Help me to remember that no challenge is too great for Your love and power. Strengthen my faith that I may stand firm amid the storms of life, knowing You are my refuge and shield. Grant me the serenity to accept the things I cannot change, courage to change the things I can, and wisdom to discern the difference. May I emerge from these trials stronger, closer to You, and more resilient in spirit. In Jesus' name I pray, amen.*

Listening Time

Now pray, "Holy Spirit, what are You saying to me?" Use the space provided, or a journal or notebook, to write what He reveals to you.

_____

_____

Trials teach us what we are; they dig up the soil, and let us see what we are made of.
—CHARLES SPURGEON

Count it all joy, my brothers, when you meet trials of various kinds.
—JAMES 1:2, ESV

FEAR NOT; TRUST GOD

I DON'T KNOW ABOUT you, but the more I study the Bible and read about Jesus' interactions with the disciples, the more patience I have as a leader. I mean, these dudes walked and talked with Jesus, breathed the same air, and still struggled with fear and lack of faith. The following account is a case in point.

> Now when He got into a boat, His disciples fol-
> lowed Him. And suddenly a great tempest arose
> on the sea, so that the boat was covered with the
> waves. But He was asleep. Then His disciples
> came to Him and awoke Him, saying, "Lord, save
> us! We are perishing!"
> But He said to them, "Why are you fearful, O
> you of little faith?" Then He arose and rebuked
> the winds and the sea, and there was a great calm.
> So the men marveled, saying, "Who can this be,
> that even the winds and the sea obey Him?"
> —MATTHEW 8:23–27, NKJV

I have seen memes on social media where people say that in this passage Jesus showed us what to do in a storm—sleep.

Well, I know firsthand that is easier said than done. Storms will try your faith. You may have heard or read about my real-life storm, but it is relevant, so I feel led to share it again.

In August 2017 the Weather Channel warned Houston over several days, "A storm is coming! A storm is coming!" The funny thing is, everyone in the Gulf area had sighed with relief when Hurricane Harvey was downgraded from a hurricane to a tropical storm. We figured, "How bad could it be?"

When Harvey actually arrived, that wishful thinking vanished. Having restrengthened to hurricane status, a slow-moving Harvey squatted over our city, dumping up to 60 inches of rainfall across four days and leaving Houston drowned in muddy, brown floodwaters that showed no sign of receding.

Earlier that day I had watched through our living room window as neighbor after neighbor left with the few belongings they could gather quickly. The water in the street was thigh high. By 2 p.m. the next day, the bayou behind our apartment building was swollen with floodwater. Brackish water sloshed a foot deep onto our patio, and I knew it was time to go. Somebody pounded on our front door, confirming my thoughts: "It's time to leave!" a voice shouted. "Grab a few things and go!"

I made several calls, and a friend from the church we pastor, Get Wrapped Church, came in a rescue boat to pick us up. Our journey across Houston took a meandering route that day. First a boat, then a van, then another boat, and finally a truck took us to our church building, which would become a major relief distribution center over the next month. As I sat in the rescue boat, my arms around my wife, Ruthy, the irony hit me: the raincoat on my back read "Noah's Ark." It was a gift from a radio station for a show I guest-hosted. Now the full weight of that irony and what we would face in the days ahead settled over me.

"God, I'm going to lose everything," I murmured into the damp air. His response was a sobering one. The Lord was like, "You are?" We had one carry-on suitcase and one backpack—from what I could tell, that was everything we now owned in the world. But when we returned home three days later, we discovered that while all the apartment buildings around us were flooded, our building was untouched. Our furniture never even got wet. It was all God because everything else around us was underwater.

During that time I learned a lot about storms that applies to our lives today.

First, *storms are unpredictable*. You don't know when they are coming. They are like a surprise party for someone who hates surprises.

Next, *many storms are unavoidable*. Unless you have plenty of advance warning, you cannot always avoid the storm or its effects. You must tap into your faith and trust God to carry you through it, as He protected us in Houston.

Third, never forget that *Jesus is in the boat with you*. You can scream, cry, and pray, but God expects you to believe He will get you through it. There is a point where the Lord expects us to release fear and fully embrace faith in Christ. Jesus expects you to spend enough time with Him and know enough scriptures to understand that He will never leave or forsake you.

Finally, God wants you to know that *He can completely calm every storm you face*. Therefore, you can confidently sleep through the storm because God is with you. No matter how loud the winds howl or how hard the rain pours down, Jesus is right there with you and will keep you safe in the midst of it all, just as He has promised.

SPIRITUAL FREEDOM STUDY

Reflect on Jesus' words in Matthew 8:26 (NKJV):

> He said to them, "Why are you fearful, O you
> of little faith?" Then He arose and rebuked the
> winds and the sea, and there was a great calm.

List three things you learned from today's reading and explain how you will use those lessons the next time you face a spiritual storm.

1. _____

_____

_____

2. _____

_____

_____

3. _____

_____

_____

Questions for Reflection

How can the assurance of God's presence and His command to "Fear not" empower you to break free from the chains of fear and experience spiritual freedom?

_____

_____

What specific areas of your life can be transformed by trusting in His unwavering love and guidance?

_____

_____

Prayer Time (Talk to Him)

> *Heavenly Father, I come before You with a heart burdened by fear and anxiety, seeking Your peace and freedom. Lord, I confess that fear has often held me captive, limiting my trust in Your sovereignty and love. Teach me to stand firm on Your promises, knowing that You are always with me, no matter the circumstances. May Your perfect love cast out all fear from my heart. In Jesus' name, amen.*

Listening Time

Now pray, "Holy Spirit, what are You saying to me?" Use the space provided, or a journal or notebook, to write what He reveals to you.

_____

_____

Meet your fears with faith.
—Max Lucado
Fear is a self-imposed prison that will keep
you from becoming what God intends
for you to be. You must move against it
with the weapons of faith and love.
—Rick Warren

Day 17

FREEDOM THROUGH DISCIPLESHIP

MANY PEOPLE DON'T know what it actually means to be a disciple. A disciple is someone who is learning, growing, and maturing in Christ. Discipleship is among the spiritual practices that separate those who praise the Lord and pray before bed from those who have a fully formed relationship with Jesus.

To obtain this, you must be willing to deny yourself and lose who you are to become more like Christ. This is what Jesus said in Luke 14:33: *"In the same way, those of you who do not give up everything you have cannot be my disciples."*

Understanding discipleship is the first step to growing closer to the Father. Why? Because you can't begin a journey you don't fully comprehend.

Discipleship is not just a series of good deeds such as going to church and singing worship songs, though those are great things. Instead, it involves studying God's Word and applying it to your life so you will bear fruit. That fruit is not just for you, even though you benefit from it. You bear fruit so others can eat from the tree of your life. That looks like sharing what you've learned with others and actually walking and doing life with them.

114

First Corinthians 4:15 says there are many teachers and few fathers. In other words, there are tons of teachings and online classes, and though those are great, we still need a day-to-day example of what it looks like to live out those truths. You can tell someone to be a good father, but it still needs to be modeled in front of that person.

This is what Jesus did. He said in Matthew 16:24–25, "If anyone wishes to come after Me, he must deny himself, and take up his cross and follow Me. For whoever wishes to save his life will lose it; but whoever loses his life for My sake will find it" (NASB). He asked us to deny ourselves and give our lives for His sake, and then He did that very thing. *Wow!*

Jesus came into the world fully man and fully God and taught us the rules of a whole other kingdom. Our natural way doesn't work in the kingdom of God. When we lay down our will and our ways—our very lives—to walk with Jesus as His disciples, we live in the truth, and that truth gives us freedom. I know dying so we can live may sound backward, but trust me, it's right!

Walter Henrichsen wrote a great book called *Disciples Are Made Not Born: Helping Others Grow to Maturity in Christ.* In it he wrote this:

> When Cortez landed at Vera Cruz in 1519 to begin his dramatic conquest of Mexico with a pocket-sized force of 700 men, he purposely set fire to his fleet of eleven ships. His men on the shore watched their only means of retreat sinking to the bottom of the Gulf of Mexico. With no means of retreat, there was only one direction in

which to move forward into the Mexican interior
to meet whatever might come their way.

In paying the price for being Christ's disciple,
you too must purposefully destroy all avenues of
retreat. Resolve in your heart today that whatever
the price for being His follower, you are willing to
pay it. Either that, or send your ambassador and
sue for peace.[1]

Being a disciple of Jesus is an all-or-nothing proposition. If
you desire to have a fruitful relationship with God and be a
good disciple, there are three relationships you should strive
to obtain. The first is someone who will pour into you. This
is any person whose relationship helps you walk with God
through your most challenging days—a mentor. Disciples
make disciples, so you need someone discipling you!

There are many reasons you need a person like this in your
life, from providing emotional support and physical protection
to simply having someone by your side no matter what. There
will be times when your faith is put to the test. When this
happens, it is critical that you have companions who push you
in the right direction so you can keep moving forward.

Consider Esther and her cousin Mordecai. If you are
unfamiliar with their story, I recommend reading the Book
of Esther in your spare time. It's only ten chapters. When
Mordecai warned Esther about a criminal plot against their
community, Esther courageously took action. Though it could
have cost her life, Esther listened to her mentor, Mordecai, and
was influential in saving her people from annihilation. This is
the type of trustworthy partnership we all need in our lives.

As a disciple the second relationship you'll need is someone who sharpens you as you sharpen them. Proverbs 27:17 says, "As iron sharpens iron, so one person sharpens another." The verse is telling us that a sharp thing can only be sharpened by something similar to itself. For example, if you're running a race with people half your speed, you will naturally slow yourself down because there's no need to use your full potential. However, if you're racing people faster than you, their speed will cause you to push yourself to keep up.

When you surround yourself with people who run slowly, you dim your talent and eventually lose the ability to tap into your full potential. That is why seeking people who push you to be your best is essential—and another valuable aspect of discipleship. The people you choose to hang around can indirectly determine the bounds of your lifelong success. If you put yourself around those who live above their means and make reckless decisions, you too will struggle to find stability. These same people will try to drag you away from your goals so you can be like them. Likewise, 1 Corinthians 15:33 says, "Do not be misled: 'Bad company corrupts good character.'" Remember this when you choose who will sharpen your iron. That one decision may seem insignificant, but it can play a leading role in your life.

The last of the three relationships is a person that you disciple. The biblical story of Samuel, a miracle child, and his mentor, Eli, is a prime example of the importance of pouring into others. First Samuel 3 tells of a young boy being sent off to learn the ways of the prophets. Throughout his years Samuel learned to listen to God and use the prophetic gift God had given him.

One night, the Lord called to Samuel three times. Each time, Samuel got up and ran to Eli, thinking he was the one who had spoken. After the third time, Eli realized what Samuel needed to do. He instructed Samuel, "Go and lie down, and if he calls you, say, 'Speak, LORD, for your servant is listening'" (1 Sam. 3:9). By doing this, Samuel opened himself to the will and voice of God.

Finally what the Lord was attempting to convey to Samuel became clear. When Eli got up, Samuel told him what the Lord had spoken—great sorrow was coming that would impact his family. Instead of resisting the word of the Lord, Eli accepted God's will, and Samuel learned to trust in God through the example set by his mentor.

We all need people who will support and aid us in life. These three relationships—someone who pours into us, someone who sharpens us, and someone whom we disciple—are keys to helping us become spiritually refreshed. As we build up others, our mentors hold us accountable. Likewise our "across," or peer-to-peer, relationships help us serve others better.

If we desire to be Christ's disciples, we cannot stand for being fleshly Christians who focus on flashy works and avoid quality relationships and conversations. Instead we should strive for authenticity. We will face hardships, but we can rely on our communities to strengthen us during those trying times. The biblical examples discussed today and many others illustrate that companionship is vital for discipleship. When you have someone lifting you up during the storm, it makes the journey that much more manageable.

SPIRITUAL FREEDOM STUDY

Read John 6:26–70, reflecting particularly on verses 66–69:

> From this time many of his disciples turned back and no longer followed him.
>
> "You do not want to leave too, do you?" Jesus asked the Twelve.
>
> Simon Peter answered him, "Lord, to whom shall we go? You have the words of eternal life. We have come to believe and to know that you are the Holy One of God."

Discipleship is a journey that we do not walk alone. It involves a community of believers who support and teach one another and grow together. By embracing these godly relationships, we find the strength and guidance to walk faithfully with Christ, no matter the challenges we face.

Questions for Reflection

Jesus calls us to give up everything to be His disciples. Consider what this means in the context of your life. Are there areas you are holding back and not fully committing to Christ? True discipleship requires complete surrender and a willingness to be molded by God's will. Think about how you can deepen your commitment to following Jesus today.

_____

_____

Consider the people who sharpen you as iron sharpens iron. Are your relationships encouraging you to grow in Christ, or are they pulling you away from Him? Are your relationships encouraging you toward spiritual growth and Christlike character?

_____

_____

Whom has God placed in your life for you to guide and mentor? How can you pour into their lives, helping them to grow in faith and obedience to God?

_____

_____

Prayer Time (Talk to Him)

> *Heavenly Father, help me to embrace the true essence of discipleship. Give me the strength to surrender all that I am and all that I have to You, trusting in Your perfect plan for my life. Show me how I can guide and support others in their spiritual journey. Help me to be a mentor who reflects Your love, wisdom, and grace. In Jesus' name, amen.*

Listening Time

Now pray, "Holy Spirit, what are You saying to me?" Use the space provided, or a journal or notebook, to write what He reveals to you.

_____

_____

*We have suffered from the preaching of
cheap grace. Grace is free, but it is not cheap.
People will take anything that is free, but
they are not interested in discipleship. They
will take Christ as Savior but not as Lord.*
—VANCE HAVNER

*Christianity without discipleship is
always Christianity without Christ.*
—DIETRICH BONHOEFFER

REPOSITION YOUR THINKING

UNTIL YOUR REVELATION becomes greater than your environment, you will remain imprisoned. When it comes to repositioning your thinking, perspective is everything.

I was writing this during the Christmas holidays, so a story that came to mind when considering the importance of perspective was the tale of Ebenezer Scrooge, whose life was dull and gray until three ghosts visited him.[1] I read an interesting essay that ascribed symbolic meaning to each ghost that visited Ebenezer. First came the Ghost of Christmas Past. He had a glowing head, symbolizing the mind and representing Ebenezer's memories. Next was the Ghost of Christmas Present; he represented the generosity and empathy that characterize what people call "the Christmas spirit." Then finally, Ebenezer was visited by the Ghost of Christmas Future, who represented the fear of death and moral reckoning.[2]

Through these visits from the ghosts, Ebenezer discovered his devious ways were negatively impacting himself and those around him. Further, he realized the only way to live a happy and fulfilled life was to be joyful and giving. Ebenezer was rich in finances yet poor in joy. His perspective of life was negative, and it caused him to be a miserable human being. The visits from those three ghosts dramatically transformed his point of view.[3]

Another example of a perspective problem is found in the Book of Numbers. Twelve spies were sent to scout out the Promised Land. All twelve went to the same place, but Caleb and Joshua saw something very different from the others. In this passage Caleb speaks up:

> But Caleb quieted the people before Moses and said, "Let us go up at once and occupy it, for we are well able to overcome it." Then the men who had gone up with him said, "We are not able to go up against the people, for they are stronger than we are." So they brought to the people of Israel a bad report of the land that they had spied out, saying, "The land, through which we have gone to spy it out, is a land that devours its inhabitants, and all the people that we saw in it are of great height. And there we saw the Nephilim (the sons of Anak, who come from the Nephilim), and we seemed to ourselves like grasshoppers, and so we seemed to them."
>
> —NUMBERS 13:30–33, ESV

Caleb and Joshua believed they could take the land and were ready to work to receive the promise; the others, however, did not. Those ten doubtful spies said three things that fully displayed their perspective problem:

1. The people are stronger than we are.

2. The people are bigger than we are.

3. We are grasshoppers in our own eyes, and we look the same to them.

The utterly crazy thing to me about this is that there is no mention of any encounter in which the land's inhabitants called them grasshoppers. The doubters' negative self-image paralyzed them and kept them from taking action and receiving the abundance God had promised and planned for them. Their improper assessment shows us that *perception matters*.

You will never seize a life of abundance if you do not see yourself properly and transform your mindset. I once heard business growth consultant Myron Golden, PhD, tell a group of entrepreneurs, "You can't win the game 'cause you ain't in the game." I thought, "Whoa. That is a word for everybody!" I know you know what I'm talking about.

Have you ever known someone who got mad about not getting a position at work, but you later found out they never applied for it? I have, and I was shocked when I found out because I realized this person wanted the position to be given to him. He wanted the boss to read his mind and know he was interested!

We have to see ourselves and the situations around us correctly. The truth of the matter is the person who did not apply for the job either was afraid of being rejected and not getting the position or never believed he deserved it in the first place. Don't let that be you! You are a child of the Most High God. You are worthy, and you were designed with a purpose. I pray that through these twenty-one days every chain will break off your life, and you will be free in Jesus to become the best version of yourself.

The best way to fix your perception is to deal with the stuff you don't like in your life so you can show up and be your most confident self. If you are dissatisfied with your weight or nutrition, I encourage you to act. If you are tired of your current financial situation, I encourage you to do something about it. Suppose you believe God has something extraordinary for you but it will take work to obtain it. In that case, I implore you to armor up and put the work in until you obtain your promise. Doing the work creates stability, and stability empowers you to keep growing and expanding.

So not only does our *perspective* matter, but our *perception* of ourselves is vital.

Finally, becoming a *problem solver* repositions your thinking in a critical way. To identify a solution, you must do the following.

1. Identify the problem.

2. Design a plan to fix it.

3. Execute the plan. (Take action.)

4. Achieve resolution.

The ten spies failed to offer solutions to the issues they saw with possessing the Promised Land. When your mind is transformed and made new in Christ, you see problems as opportunities. I know David is often used as an example in books and sermons, but here is another instance where David illustrates a point well. Let's take a look:

One of the Israelite men said, "Did you see that man? Look at him! He comes out each day and makes fun of Israel. Whoever kills him will get rich. King Saul will give him a lot of money. Saul will also let his daughter marry the man who kills Goliath. He will also make that man's family free from taxes in Israel."

David asked the men standing near him, "What did he say? What is the reward for killing this Philistine and taking away this shame from Israel? Who is this Goliath anyway? He is only some foreigner, nothing but a Philistine. Why does he think he can speak against the army of the living God?"

So the Israelite told David about the reward for killing Goliath. David's oldest brother Eliab heard David talking with the soldiers and became angry. Eliab asked David, "Why did you come here? Who did you leave those few sheep with in the desert? I know why you came down here. You didn't want to do what you were told to do. You just wanted to come down here to watch the battle."

David said, "What did I do now? I didn't do anything wrong! I was only talking."

—1 SAMUEL 17:25–29, ERV

Not only did David volunteer to solve the most challenging problem his nation was facing, but he also ensured he

understood the benefits of handling the crisis. While everyone
else was focused on the size of the problem, David zeroed in
on the fact that God would be with him and the rewards that
would come with defeating the enemy.

Our perspective can be our greatest asset or our most
significant hindrance. When we align our thoughts with God's
promises, we open ourselves to a world of possibilities. Let us
choose to be like Joshua, Caleb, and David, who saw through
the lens of faith and trusted in God. In doing so, we can move
mountains and claim the victories God has in store for us.

SPIRITUAL FREEDOM STUDY

I encourage you to memorize Philippians 4:6–7:

> Do not be anxious about anything, but in every
> situation, by prayer and petition, with thanks-
> giving, present your requests to God. And the
> peace of God, which transcends all understanding,
> will guard your hearts and your minds in Christ
> Jesus.

In life I have realized that giants or things that seem big
to us (impossibilities) are small to God. By memorizing this
passage you can remind yourself to not let anything cause
anxiety, but to exchange your earthly worries for a heavenly
result through prayer. When we give thanks, we are inviting
God into our situation. And then peace will enter because our
praise and thanksgiving remind us that God is perfect and He's
got it handled, which puts our minds at ease!

Question for Reflection

What giant are you facing today, and how can you reposition your thinking to see this challenge as an opportunity for growth and victory in Christ?

_____

_____

Prayer Time (Talk to Him)

> *Heavenly Father, renew my mind so that I see myself as You see me. Replace my doubts with Your truth and my fears with Your assurance. In Jesus' name, amen.*

Listening Time

Now pray, "Holy Spirit, what are You saying to me?" Use the space provided, or a journal or notebook, to write what He reveals to you.

_____

_____

*The safest place in all the world is in
the will of God, and the safest protection
in all the world is the name of God.*
—WARREN W. WIERSBE

*David was the last one we would have chosen
to fight the giant, but he was chosen of God.*
—DWIGHT L. MOODY

Day 19

INVITED TO THE TABLE

IN THE BOOK of Luke, Jesus tells the well-known story of the prodigal son. The main characters are a father and his two sons. The younger son asked his father for his share of the estate. Without protest the father divided his estate and gave the younger son his share. The son liquidated his entire portion and quickly squandered the money, living a life of indulgence. With nothing left of his inheritance, he ended up working as a hired hand for a pig farmer.

> When he came to his senses, he said, "How many of my father's hired servants have food to spare, and here I am starving to death! I will set out and go back to my father and say to him: Father, I have sinned against heaven and against you. I am no longer worthy to be called your son; make me like one of your hired servants." So he got up and went to his father.
>
> But while he was still a long way off, his father saw him and was filled with compassion for him; he ran to his son, threw his arms around him and kissed him.
>
> The son said to him, "Father, I have sinned

131

against heaven and against you. I am no longer worthy to be called your son."

But the father said to his servants, "Quick! Bring the best robe and put it on him. Put a ring on his finger and sandals on his feet. Bring the fattened calf and kill it. Let's have a feast and celebrate. For this son of mine was dead and is alive again; he was lost and is found." So they began to celebrate.

Meanwhile, the older son was in the field. When he came near the house, he heard music and dancing. So he called one of the servants and asked him what was going on. "Your brother has come," he replied, "and your father has killed the fattened calf because he has him back safe and sound."

The older brother became angry and refused to go in. So his father went out and pleaded with him. But he answered his father, "Look! All these years I've been slaving for you and never disobeyed your orders. Yet you never gave me even a young goat so I could celebrate with my friends. But when this son of yours who has squandered your property with prostitutes comes home, you kill the fattened calf for him!"

"My son," the father said, "you are always with me, and everything I have is yours. But we had to celebrate and be glad, because this brother of

> yours was dead and is alive again; he was lost and
> is found."
>
> —LUKE 15:17–32

After sleeping and eating with the pigs, the son eventually returned to his father's home, hoping to be embraced again. Upon the son's arrival, his father welcomed him with open arms, but his brother wanted nothing to do with him.

Ultimately the story highlights that God does indeed seek sinners. Everybody is invited to the Lord's table, no matter their past. Sinners include lost sons, gay people, drug addicts, prisoners, prostitutes—Jesus invites all to come to Him.

We must remember that Jesus sat with sinners. We see this in Mark 2 when Jesus had dinner with tax collectors and others considered less desirable.

> When the teachers of the law who were Pharisees
> saw him eating with the sinners and tax collectors,
> they asked his disciples: "Why does he eat with
> tax collectors and sinners?"
>
> On hearing this, Jesus said to them, "It is not
> the healthy who need a doctor, but the sick. I have
> not come to call the righteous, but sinners."
>
> —MARK 2:16–17

The righteous must understand that no one needs a doctor when they are healthy. The sick value the doctor's help the most. This is why the father received his prodigal son so warmly; his lost son had been found; his "sick" son was coming home to be healed.

The story of the prodigal son reminds us that anyone can be redeemed—*everyone* is invited to the table. We can attempt to fulfill all the "right" religious duties, but if we don't possess love, we aren't living out the heart of the Father. We see this reminder in John 13:34: "A new commandment I give to you, that you love one another: just as I have loved you, you also are to love one another" (ESV). God has always expected us to love one another as He has loved us, without exceptions, in a pure, unfiltered way. The father's love for his lost son exemplifies this.

To judge and renounce others because they hold differing views is not righteous. God does not show favoritism. It is dangerous for self-righteous people to exclude others from the table. We should remove this way of thinking and learn to invite everyone to the feet of Jesus. The older brother in the parable struggled with this spirit of judgment. After he heard about his father's excitement over his brother's return, he was disgusted. The Bible says the brother lashed out at his father, but his father humbly replied: "My son...you are always with me, and everything I have is yours. But we had to celebrate and be glad, because this brother of yours was dead and is alive again; he was lost and is found" (Luke 15:31–32).

Much can be learned from this exchange. First, we must understand that unaddressed emotions weigh on the offender and the offended. If you're ever wondering why you're still in the same place you were a decade ago, ask yourself if you're holding on to pain from the past. Forgiveness isn't about the person being forgiven; it's for you. The older brother was disappointed that his sibling was not held accountable for his actions. He thought his brother should have faced repercussions for being irresponsible and his father should have celebrated him instead for his faithfulness. Instead, the father rejoiced that his younger son had turned from sin and reminded his older son that he already had access to all his possessions—he just hadn't asked for them.

The parable teaches us that although one son walked away from the light, both sons were lost in different ways. They were both searching for something they already had at home: acceptance. Their father loved each of them, but they had to experience something to be restored to the table. The younger son learned that the grass is not always greener on the other side. The older son learned that he had not because he asked not. (See James 4:2–3.)

God knows what He's doing. One person being blessed with what you *want* doesn't mean God isn't giving you what you *need*. His plan is complex; it has twists and turns, mountains and valleys. What others possess should not concern you because you serve a deliberate God. It is easy to miss out on what He is trying to give you, so focus on your walk with God and no one else's. Understand your life will come together according to God's will and timing.

If you ever feel you've strayed too far, understand that God knows our imperfections and loves us anyway. It is never too late to come home; it is never too late to reposition yourself at the table. Proof of this is found in the Bible's most important story: Jesus' crucifixion. Christ died so our imperfections wouldn't disqualify us from knowing Him. Jesus didn't just die for some—He died for all.

We are all sinners and fall short of God's glory (Rom. 3:23). Just as we all need regular *checkups* with our physicians, our relationship with God must be monitored daily. Like a house requires tending to stay beautiful and habitable, we must commune with God daily. This is not an activity you partake in only on Sundays at church or Wednesdays at Bible study. Every day should be given to the Lord, since without Him waking you up, you wouldn't be here to see another day. A heart full of gratitude is better positioned to receive the medicine we all need to be in good, righteous health: God's grace and mercy.

Remember, true freedom and healing begin with understanding and accepting the love and grace Jesus offers.

SPIRITUAL FREEDOM STUDY

Consider the story of the prodigal son, paying special attention to Luke 15:17–20:

> When he came to his senses, he said, "How many of my father's hired servants have food to spare, and here I am starving to death! I will set out and go back to my father and say to him: Father, I have sinned against heaven and against you. I am no longer worthy to be called your son; make me like one of your hired servants." So he got up and went to his father. But while he was still a long way off, his father saw him and was filled with compassion for him; he ran to his son, threw his arms around him and kissed him.

Jesus' teachings challenge us to redefine our perspectives—to see ourselves, others, and even God in a new light. Whether we identify with the prodigal son or the elder brother, the invitation is the same: to come home to the Father's love. Let's respond to this call, embracing the joy of Jesus' feast and the new life He offers.

Question for Reflection

How can you step into the fullness of your identity in Christ, living out the reality of being a beloved child of God, and extend that same grace and love to others around you?

_____

_____

Prayer Time (Talk to Him)

Heavenly Father, thank You for making me a new creation in Christ. Help me to live out this truth, showing the world Your love and grace through my life. Guide me to be an ambassador of Your reconciliation. In Jesus' name, amen.

Listening Time

Now pray, "Holy Spirit, what are You saying to me?" Use the space provided, or a journal or notebook, to write what He reveals to you.

_____

_____

The difference between mercy and grace?
Mercy gave the prodigal son a second
chance. Grace gave him a feast.
—MAX LUCADO

We must learn how to repent of the sin
under all our other sins and under all our
righteousness—the sin of seeking to be our
own Savior and Lord. We must admit that
we've put our ultimate hope and trust in
things other than God, and that in both our
wrongdoing and right doing we have been
seeking to get around God or get control of
God in order to get hold of those things.
—TIMOTHY KELLER

TAKING THOUGHTS CAPTIVE

T HE TRANSFORMATIVE POWER of Christ can turn a chaotic
life into a testimony of God's amazing grace. Today we will
dive into the practice of taking every thought captive, a vital
step in breaking free from the strongholds that bind us.

The Bible tells us that our spiritual warfare requires divine
weapons.

> The weapons of our warfare are not physical
> [weapons of flesh and blood]. Our weapons are
> divinely powerful for the destruction of fortresses.
> We are destroying sophisticated arguments and
> every exalted and proud thing that sets itself up
> against the [true] knowledge of God, and we are
> taking every thought and purpose captive to the
> obedience of Christ.
> —2 CORINTHIANS 10:4–5, AMP

The weapons of our warfare are not of this world but are
mighty in God for pulling down strongholds. Think about your
life. Have negative thoughts, patterns, or behaviors created
fortresses? Do you find yourself overwhelmed by anxiety,
insecurity, or feelings of inferiority? Do you often think you're

not smart enough, talented enough, or important enough to pursue the things you desire? Do you think you can't break that habit or that you'll never be able to change a certain behavior? Those are lies from the enemy! Commit to using the truth of God's Word as your primary weapon to break these strongholds.

If anyone is qualified to talk about taking thoughts captive and the benefits of doing so, I certainly am. Until a radical encounter with Jesus behind prison walls, all I did was sow death. As a matter of fact, for twenty-three years my life was full of stealing, killing, and destroying. However, by God's grace my life has drastically changed, and I now have a deep, burning passion to sow life where death once prevailed. I live with a purpose—to bring His marvelous light into the darkest places and fill the earth with the glory of God.

Instead of being busy with back-alley business and courtroom appearances, I now busy myself with crusades and street revivals. I'm humbled to say that my testimony is touching people powerfully around the world as it proclaims the truth of the gospel through a redeemed heart. A testimony is the statement of a witness under oath, so our testimonies attest to what God has done in our lives as we tell the story of how we overcame.

For me, change started when I began demolishing strongholds and taking my thought life captive to the Word of God. Maybe you are thinking, "Yo, Pastor Juan, I am new to this Bible thing. What does 'demolishing strongholds' mean?" Well, hold tight. I am going to break it down.

When I say "demolish strongholds," I mean that we are tearing down spiritual, mental, emotional, and psychological walls; wrong thought patterns; and destructive behaviors.

There are many ways strongholds can present themselves in someone's life. In the Bible, strongholds are represented in two ways: either as fortresses meant to protect us in times of trouble or as harmful thought patterns, arrogant attitudes, or messages from the outside world that have left a lasting impression on our minds and hearts. When it comes to the latter definition, earthly limitations get locked inside the fortress with us, and the only way to eradicate them from our lives is to remove ourselves from the stronghold.

Many strongholds have become so powerful because they are ingrained in our routines and habits, which can create complacency, apathy, and lack of control. So to be clear, when I talk about strongholds, I am not only talking about sin. I am also talking about habits and behaviors that displease God and push you away from having a deeper relationship with Him.

For example, procrastination is a cousin of laziness that we don't like to discuss, even though the Word clearly calls it out. Proverbs 13:4 tells us that "the soul of the sluggard craves and gets nothing, while the soul of the diligent is richly supplied" (ESV). This verse means those who are lazy and crave a lot will receive nothing, while those who work diligently will be richly supplied and satisfied through the Lord.

Strongholds can be anything from holding on to a relationship that was meant for only a season to abusing drugs and alcohol. Anything that shackles you and prevents you from genuinely conforming to God and His will needs to be cast out of your life. The truth is, when you are dead to sin, you're alive to God. Though I've done some *crazy* things in my life, God has delivered me from my old ways of thinking. None of my old

habits or desires exist anymore. Isn't that weird? When I committed to His process, my whole life changed.

When you attempt to abandon your strongholds yourself,
you may not be strong enough, which can make you feel like
the task is impossible. The devil wants you trapped in the sin
that burdens you the most because it distracts you from the
Lord. So remember to continue fighting the good fight until
you are free instead of perpetuating a sinful or unproductive
cycle. That doesn't have to be your life! Jesus died on the cross
so you and I can have abundant life in heaven and here on earth.

I want to share five keys to taking your thoughts captive and
demolishing strongholds in your life.

1. Take responsibility. Have you ever been in a house with
a lot of people, especially kids, and something gets broken, but
nobody knows how it got broken? Ugh, that drives me crazy
because we know the item did not break itself. Well, I believe
our Father in heaven is waiting to help us fix the broken areas
in our lives, but we must take responsibility. Acknowledge and
own up to your thoughts, actions, and deeds—this is the first
step to owning your part. Stop lying to yourself! I always tell
my kids, "If you lie to yourself, you will lie to everyone else." *Be
honest!* Remember that transformation begins with the renewal
of your mind. Reflect on how your thoughts influence your
actions, and align them with God's will.

2. Understand the mind-body connection. I remember
asking a youth pastor how he talks to his youth about abstaining
from premarital sex, and he gave me the most brilliant answer.
He said he tells them to "date in public" and stay away from
anywhere they can get comfortable lying down. Dating in
public kept them from being alone, which lessened the chances

of intimacy. The second part had them avoiding places with back seats, couches, bleachers, and beds. The idea was to create as many barriers as possible to doing the wrong thing and as many positive opportunities to do the right thing. Your mind and your actions must work together if you are going to be obedient to the Word of God.

3. Take time to respond. Sometimes we fall into sin because we are too quick to respond, reply, or react to something that happens in our lives. When we take time to pray and seek wise counsel, we will get better results and face less hardship.

4. Confess your sins. God encourages us to confess to Him and one another. Now, you should not be telling everyone your deepest secrets and troubles. Still, you should have intercessors and other like-minded believers praying with you when you are going through difficult seasons. Remember, confessing to God includes coming into agreement with what He has to say about a matter. You must agree that something is sinful before you can confess it as a sin.

5. Realize this is a spiritual battle. Please never forget that even though people may oppose or hurt you, you are not wrestling with flesh and blood. The enemy uses people to do his deeds on earth. And because Satan is the prince of the power of the air and the ruler of the darkness of this world, sometimes the battles we face have nothing to do with the people who agitate or attack us and everything to do with the enemy trying to keep us bound.

You can only fight this battle spiritually. Although I wish I could punch the devil in the face in the physical, I can only punch him in the heavenly realm, where the battle is. Read Ephesians 6:10–18 and accept that word! Recognize the spiritual nature of our battles. Our fight is not against people but against spiritual forces. Equip yourself with the full armor of God, understanding that victory comes through the Lord. Contemplate how you can actively engage in this spiritual battle through prayer, Scripture reading, and righteous living.

SPIRITUAL FREEDOM STUDY

Taking every thought captive is more than a mental exercise; it's a spiritual discipline. By surrendering our thoughts to Christ, we break free from the enemy's lies and step into the freedom of God's truth. Let us continually seek to renew our minds and live as victorious disciples of Christ. Remember, your thoughts and beliefs drive your behavior.

Meditate on Romans 12:1–2:

> Therefore, I urge you, brothers and sisters, in view of God's mercy, to offer your bodies as a living sacrifice, holy and pleasing to God—this is your true and proper worship. Do not conform to the pattern of this world, but be transformed by the renewing of your mind. Then you will be able to test and approve what God's will is—his good, pleasing and perfect will.

Commit to a daily practice of renewing your mind through Scripture reading and prayer.

Questions for Reflection

Reflect on the areas of your life in which you struggle to maintain godly thoughts and attitudes. What specific steps can you take daily to align these thoughts with the teachings of Christ and cultivate a mindset that honors God?

_____

_____

How can you reinforce these steps with prayer and Scripture to ensure they become a natural part of your spiritual discipline?

_____

_____

Prayer Time (Talk to Him)

Heavenly Father, thank You for showing me the path to true freedom through the discipline of taking every thought captive to obey Christ. Lord, help me to remain steadfast in this spiritual battle, using the divine weapons You have provided to tear down strongholds and align my thoughts with Your truth.

Grant me the wisdom to discern the lies of the enemy and the courage to confront them with the authority of Your Word. May my mind be continually renewed and my actions reflect Your will and purpose for my life.

I ask for Your guidance and the Holy Spirit's conviction as I strive to live a life that is pleasing to You, free from the bonds of worldly thinking. May Your peace, which surpasses all understanding, guard my heart and mind in Christ Jesus. In Jesus' name, amen.

Listening Time

Now pray, "Holy Spirit, what are You saying to me?" Use the space provided, or a journal or notebook, to write what He reveals to you.

_____

_____

Our lives are always moving in the
direction of our strongest thoughts.
What we think shapes who we are.
—CRAIG GROESCHEL

When a person is going through a hard time,
his mind wants to give up. Satan knows that if
he can defeat us in our mind, he can defeat us
in our experience. That's why it is so important
that we not lose heart, grow weary and faint.
—JOYCE MEYER

You cannot change what you do not confront.
—CRAIG GROESCHEL

Day 21

AT HIS FEET: FINDING TRUE FREEDOM IN GOD'S PRESENCE

IN OUR BUSY, fast-paced lives, it's easy to get caught up in the doing and forget the being. Today's devotional, based on the story of Mary and Martha, invites us to take a look at true worship and the importance of prioritizing our relationship with God over our performance for Him. If you're anything like me, you need a constant reminder of this. Man, can I get busy and lose focus. But this story always helps me remember what's important—or better yet, what's most important.

> As Jesus and his disciples were on their way, he came to a village where a woman named Martha opened her home to him. She had a sister called Mary, who sat at the Lord's feet listening to what he said. But Martha was distracted by all the preparations that had to be made. She came to him and asked, "Lord, don't you care that my sister has left me to do the work by myself? Tell her to help me!"
>
> "Martha, Martha," the Lord answered, "you are worried and upset about many things, but few things are needed—or indeed only one. Mary

has chosen what is better, and it will not be taken away from her."

—LUKE 10:38–42

Look again at that last line: "'Martha, Martha,' the Lord answered, 'you are worried and upset about many things, but few things are needed—or indeed only one. Mary has chosen what is better, and it will not be taken away from her.'" Notice that Jesus said Martha's name twice. We should pause here because anything that's repeated in Scripture is essential. At this moment, Martha was being divinely corrected. Jesus repeated her name because He needed her to understand the importance of what He was about to say.

When Mary sat at Jesus' feet, she took the posture of a student receiving teaching from a superior. This was a posture of humility. Every time we see Mary in these verses she's at Jesus' feet, listening to His words. God desires us to have a constant and consistent desire to seek and worship Him genuinely.

Be wise like Mary and always open your heart and ears to receive from God. His guidance will set you on a path far more significant than any other. We learn, grow, and mature as we sit at His feet. We build a relationship with Christ when we put away our selfish desires and pay attention to Him. Nothing is more important than being in the presence of the Father.

When we release our distractions and give God our all, we come to know Him better. This is what the Lord desires. God wants everyone to know His heart. Do not be like the Pharisees and perform for God by throwing your hands up and yelling "Amen!" during church. Instead, fully relinquish yourself to the Lord and honor Him in your everyday life.

A few years ago I stumbled upon a letter I kept back in prison. The author is unknown, but I want to share the letter here because it makes the relationship Jesus wants to have with us soberingly simple.

A LETTER FROM JESUS

I'm sending you this letter by way of one of My disciples. I just want to tell you how much I love you and how much I want to be a part of your life. This morning, when you woke up, I was already there, in the warm, radiant sunshine that filled your room. I waited for you to speak to Me, but you never did. When you went out the door, I again tried to get your attention. I kissed your face with the soft, gentle breeze, and then I sang you some love songs from the birds in the trees, but you just walked on by as though I wasn't even there.

Later that day, I stood by watching as you talked and joked and laughed with your friends. I waited for you to speak to Me, but you never noticed Me. Oh, how I wish you would take a few minutes to talk to Me each day. I painted a beautiful rainbow in the sky. I just knew that you would see Me then, but you were too busy doing other things. I sent you a beautiful sunset to close out the day as you laid down to sleep. I winked at you a thousand times through the stars in the sky, hoping you would see Me. But you never noticed Me.

How I wish that you would spend a few minutes with Me before you go to sleep each night, but you never do. My dear child, it hurts Me so much for you to ignore Me. I continue to watch over you all through the night, hoping you will notice Me and speak to Me in the morning. I have revealed Myself to you in so many ways, and all I want is for you to accept Me as your Lord and Savior. For you see, I am truly the only one who can save you and provide all your needs. Please let Me hear from you real soon. I have so much to share with you. Okay. I love you.

Your friend forever and ever,

Jesus[1]

In this letter it is clear that God wants us to spend time with Him and acknowledge all He has given us. Without the sun and moon we could not exist on this planet. Without the sun there would be no light to make things grow, and without the gravitational pull from the moon, Earth would be less stable. Our lives would be dull without rainbows and stars, and there would be no food for consumption if God had not created the plants and animals we eat daily. Through nature He provides ways for us to commune with Him. Gentle breezes, rain showers, the grass under our feet, and the living things around us are all pathways to see and love our God.

I encourage you to speak to the Lord when you wake up in the morning, even if it's simply to say hello as you walk out of your house or to ask that He bless and guide you throughout the day. Consider Martha's and Mary's contrasting approaches to Jesus' presence in their home: Martha, the "spiritual workaholic," is busy "doing" while Mary chooses to just "be," sitting at Jesus' feet in a posture of learning and intimacy. Reflect on your own faith journey. Are you more like Martha, focused on serving and doing, or like Mary, prioritizing being and listening?

As you go about your day, think about Martha's complaint to Jesus and her focus on performance. It's easy to become so absorbed in serving Jesus that we forget the joy of simply being with Him. Reflect on times when your service for God has become more about your efforts than about His presence. Meditate on Jesus' gentle correction to Martha. He emphasizes that "one thing is necessary." This is a powerful reminder to prioritize our relationship with God above all else. If we're busy doing, we need to simplify our spiritual lives to focus more on being in God's presence.

SPIRITUAL FREEDOM STUDY

In a world that often values doing over being, Jesus invites us to choose the better part—to sit at His feet, learn from Him, and deepen our relationship with Him. Let's strive to be like Mary, understanding that our greatest calling is not just to work for God but to be with Him.

As you reflect on this truth, consider David's prayer in Psalm 27:4:

> One thing I ask from the LORD, this only do I
> seek: that I may dwell in the house of the LORD

all the days of my life, to gaze on the beauty of the
LORD and to seek him in his temple.

Question for Reflection

How can you create space in your busy life to sit at Jesus' feet
and listen to Him, making His presence your ultimate priority?

_____

_____

Prayer Time (Talk to Him)

*Heavenly Father, in a world that often pulls me in
countless directions and reminds me constantly of
my tasks and responsibilities, help me to find true
freedom in Your presence. Like Mary, let me choose
the better part—to sit at Your feet and listen to Your
words. Teach me, Lord, to prioritize being still and
spending time with You. In Jesus' name, amen.*

Listening Time

Now pray, "Holy Spirit, what are You saying to me?" Use the
space provided, or a journal or notebook, to write what He
reveals to you.

_____

_____

Closet communion needs time for the revelation of God's presence. It is vain to say: "I have too much work to do to find time." You must find time or forfeit blessing. God knows how to save for you the time you sacredly keep for communion with Him.
—A. T. PIERSON

Only with time do we really learn who the other person is and come to love the person for him- or herself and not just for the feelings and experiences they give us.
—TIM KELLER

The greatest enemy of good thinking is busyness.
—JOHN C. MAXWELL

FASTING AND PRAYER: TOOLS TO STRENGTHEN YOUR SPIRIT

ICREATED THIS BONUS day because I truly believe prayer and fasting are foundational disciplines we must consistently practice as believers. Fasting is where we learn how to kill the flesh to strengthen the spirit man. It is where we get power. You will never be fruitful without sacrifice (dying to self). There's a lot of talk about surrendering our lives to Christ, but there's not enough walk. We must say, like Paul, "I no longer live. It's now Christ living in me!" (See Galatians 2:20.)

The cross is the key to your fruitfulness. The power to stop the flesh is at the cross!

Let's read Matthew 6:1–13 (csb):

> Be careful not to practice your righteousness in front of others to be seen by them. Otherwise, you have no reward with your Father in heaven. So whenever you give to the poor, don't sound a trumpet before you, as the hypocrites do in the synagogues and on the streets, to be applauded by people. Truly I tell you, they have their reward.

But when you give to the poor, don't let your left hand know what your right hand is doing, so that your giving may be in secret. And your Father who sees in secret will reward you.

Whenever you pray, you must not be like the hypocrites, because they love to pray standing in the synagogues and on the street corners to be seen by people. Truly I tell you, they have their reward. But when you pray, go into your private room, shut your door, and pray to your Father who is in secret. And your Father who sees in secret will reward you. When you pray, don't babble like the Gentiles, since they imagine they'll be heard for their many words. Don't be like them, because your Father knows the things you need before you ask him.

Therefore, you should pray like this: Our Father in heaven, your name be honored as holy. Your kingdom come. Your will be done on earth as it is in heaven. Give us today our daily bread. And forgive us our debts, as we also have forgiven our debtors. And do not bring us into temptation, but deliver us from the evil one.

Prayer is cooperating with God to bring about His plan, not trying to bend Him to our will. When we don't pray, we will grow distant. When we do pray, we will not only grow closer to God but we will also become more like Him because we will be sensitive to what He values most.

Immediately after that passage in Matthew 6, Jesus goes on to talk about how to fast.

> And when you fast, do not look gloomy like the hypocrites, for they disfigure their faces that their fasting may be seen by others. Truly, I say to you, they have received their reward. But when you fast, anoint your head and wash your face, that your fasting may not be seen by others but by your Father who is in secret. And your Father who sees in secret will reward you.
>
> —MATTHEW 6:16–18, ESV

Notice that Jesus said, "*When* you fast..." He expects fasting to be part of the life of a believer. We fast from a humble heart to seek God. In Isaiah 58 the people were complaining that they had fasted but God had not responded. The Lord told them it was because their fasting had been hypocritical, done as a pretentious, outward ritual instead of in genuine humility before God.

We don't fast to manipulate God into giving us what we desire like He's some kind of genie in a bottle. We fast out of a hunger for God. It is a way to humble ourselves before Him and present ourselves as living sacrifices, as Romans 12:1 instructs. If we can't give God our stomachs, we will never give Him our bodies. Biblical fasting weakens the flesh to strengthen the spirit.

Romans 8:7 reminds us that "the mind governed by the flesh is hostile to God; it does not submit to God's law, nor can it do so." We are called to live in the realm of the Spirit, and fasting helps us in this journey. Even Jesus spent time fasting to gain strength for His calling.

Luke 4 tells us the Holy Spirit led Jesus into the wilderness, where He fasted for forty days and nights. During that time, Jesus faced relentless temptation from Satan. The devil attacked His identity as the Son of God, tried to get Him to turn stones into bread to satisfy His natural hunger, and thought he could trick Jesus into worshipping him in exchange for success and glory in the world. Jesus relied on the Word of God, not His own strength, to defeat these temptations and remain victorious over sin.

If the Son of God did not rely on His flesh to live in obedience to God, then we can't either. After Jesus was tempted, the Bible says He "returned to Galilee in the power of the Spirit" (Luke 4:14). So we see that fasting helps us draw closer to the Lord, strengthens us spiritually, and enables us to move in the power of the Spirit!

Different forms of fasting are mentioned in the Bible, including regular fasting (water only), partial fasting (some foods, such as a Daniel fast), and absolute fasting (no food or water). In 2 Chronicles 20 Jehoshaphat, the king of Judah, called a regular fast when a great multitude sought to attack the nation. The Lord spoke through a prophet that the battle was not theirs but His. And when the vast army came, the enemy soldiers fought against themselves instead of Judah until no one was left. All the people of Judah had to do was collect the spoils!

In Daniel 10 we see an example of a partial fast. Daniel "ate no choice food; no meat or wine touched [his] lips" for three weeks as he sought a word from the Lord (v. 3). He later learned in a vision that the Lord sent an angel with the answer right when he prayed, but a demonic principality resisted the angel for twenty-one days. Fasting helped bring breakthrough! Remember, the Bible tells us there are some things that "[do] not go out except by prayer and fasting" (Matt. 17:21, NKJV).

In Esther 4 we see an example of an absolute fast. She asked all the Jews in Persia not to eat or drink for three days as she prepared to see the king and ask him to spare the lives of her people. God gave her favor with the king, and not only were the people of Israel saved from annihilation, but their enemy was put to death instead.

In the Book of Joel we find yet another kind of fast, a solemn assembly where the people of Israel cried out to God corporately. Because of their faithfulness to do what God asked, the Lord promised to restore them:

> I will repay you for the years the locusts have eaten—the great locust and the young locust, the other locusts and the locust swarm—my great army that I sent among you. You will have plenty to eat, until you are full, and you will praise the name of the LORD your God, who has worked wonders for you; never again will my people be shamed.
>
> —JOEL 2:25–26

Each type of fast serves a specific purpose and can help us grow spiritually. Fasting is not just about abstaining from food; it can also involve abstaining from other physical desires such as sexual relations, as seen in Exodus 19:15 and 1 Corinthians 7:5. Keep in mind that abstaining from social media or entertainment is not fasting. That is a great thing to do while fasting because they can cause distractions. But fasting is crucifying the flesh by abstaining from food or something else our physical bodies crave.

Whatever kind of fast you engage in, prayer must be part of the equation. I've heard it said that a fast without prayer is nothing but a diet. Prayer and fasting go hand in hand; together they strengthen our spirits, humble our hearts, and draw us closer to God. As we seek Him with sincerity and humility and cooperate with His divine plan, we align our will with His and grow ever more dependent on the Lord. So let us approach prayer and fasting with sincere and humble hearts, knowing that it is a form of worship and a means to deepen our relationship with our heavenly Father.

Here's a fun fact: Did you know that during the Civil War, President Abraham Lincoln called the United States to a day of "national humiliation, fasting, and prayer"? The Civil War devastated the nation, especially the South, but a year after the war ended, in 1866, the nation experienced an economic surplus, and it continued for twenty-eight years in a row.[1] America was *blessed*, and I believe the people's willingness to humble themselves in prayer and fasting had something to do with that.

I decided to include President Lincoln's proclamation here so you can read it for yourself.

Proclamation 97—Appointing a Day of National Humiliation, Fasting, and Prayer

Whereas the Senate of the United States, devoutly recognizing the supreme authority and just government of Almighty God in all the affairs of men and of nations, has by a resolution requested the President to designate and set apart a day for national prayer and humiliation; and

Whereas it is the duty of nations as well as of men to own their dependence upon the overruling power of God, to confess their sins and transgressions in humble sorrow, yet with assured hope that genuine repentance will lead to mercy and pardon, and to recognize the sublime truth, announced in the Holy Scriptures and proven by all history, that those nations only are blessed whose God is the Lord;

And, insomuch as we know that by His divine law nations, like individuals, are subjected to punishments and chastisements in this world, may we not justly fear that the awful calamity of civil war which now desolates the land may be but a punishment inflicted upon us for our presumptuous sins, to the needful end of our national reformation as a whole people? We have been the recipients of the choicest bounties of Heaven; we have been preserved these many years in peace and prosperity; we have grown in numbers, wealth, and power as no other nation has ever grown. But we have forgotten God. We have forgotten the gracious hand which preserved us in peace and multiplied and enriched and strengthened us, and we have vainly imagined, in the deceitfulness of our hearts, that all these blessings were produced by some superior wisdom and virtue of our own. Intoxicated with unbroken success, we have become too self-sufficient to feel the necessity of redeeming and preserving grace, too proud to pray to the God that made us.

It behooves us, then, to humble ourselves before the offended Power, to confess our national sins, and to pray for clemency and forgiveness.

Now, therefore, in compliance with the request, and fully concurring in the views of the Senate, I do by this my proclamation designate and set apart Thursday, the 30th day of April, 1863, as a day of national humiliation, fasting, and prayer. And I do hereby request all the people to abstain on that day from their ordinary secular pursuits, and to unite at their several places of public worship and their respective homes in keeping the day holy to the Lord and devoted to the humble discharge of the religious duties proper to that solemn occasion.

All this being done in sincerity and truth, let us then rest humbly in the hope authorized by the divine teachings that the united cry of the nation will be heard on high and answered with blessings no less than the pardon of our national sins and the restoration of our now divided and suffering country to its former happy condition of unity and peace. In witness whereof I have hereunto set my hand and caused the seal of the United States to be affixed.

Done at the city of Washington, this 30th day of March, A.D. 1863, and of the Independence of the United States the eighty-seventh.

ABRAHAM LINCOLN.

By the President:

WILLIAM H. SEWARD, Secretary of State[2]

I wonder what would happen if we did that again. We might not be able to get the entire nation to participate, but we can start in our own lives and homes and see the benefits of prayer and fasting.

SPIRITUAL FREEDOM STUDY

Let's read the Lord's Prayer:

Pray, then, in this way: "Our Father who is in heaven, hallowed be Your name. Your kingdom come. Your will be done, on earth as it is in heaven. Give us this day our daily bread. And forgive us our debts, as we also have forgiven our debtors. And do not lead us into temptation, but deliver us from evil. [For Yours is the kingdom and the power and the glory forever. Amen."]

—MATTHEW 6:9–13, NASB

I want us to remember that this is how Jesus says we are to pray. We don't have to repeat these words verbatim. This simply provides a framework for prayer.

We must keep in mind that we are in a relationship with God. How would your spouse feel if every word you said was a quote from someone else? It wouldn't feel very personal, and your spouse would probably begin to question your love.

In a similar way, the Lord's Prayer is a guide for our prayer life. "Our Father who is in heaven, hallowed be Your name" reminds us that we are to put some respect on His name. We can't approach God like He's just anybody; He is our Father. Then, remember that in order for His will to be done, His kingdom must come. He must rule and reign over our souls. When we allow Him to be Lord of our lives, we will not pray selfish prayers. We will ask for what we need daily to fulfill His plan for His kingdom to rule in the earth. That's what prayer is about, bringing heaven on earth—not for selfish gain, since He already knows what we need, but to build His kingdom.

Questions for Reflection

Before you begin a fast, consider the following questions: Why do you feel led to fast and pray at this time in your life? What are your specific goals or intentions for this period of fasting and prayer? What areas of your life need to be better aligned with God's will? What form of fasting are you called to? What will your ongoing prayer and fasting practices look like beyond this specific period? How can you continue to cultivate a lifestyle of prayer and dependence on God?

Remember, abstaining from entertainment or social media is not fasting, though that is a great way to avoid distractions while fasting. Also, be sure to read the Word and pray during your fast.

_____

_____

Prayer Time (Talk to Him)

> *Heavenly Father, I honor and adore Your name. May Your loving and just rule extend into every aspect of my life, aligning my desires with Your perfect will here on earth. I trust You to provide for my daily needs, both the physical and the spiritual, as I seek to follow Your path.*
>
> *Forgive me when I fall short, and help me to extend that same forgiveness to those who may have wronged me. Guide me away from the trials and challenges that could lead me astray, and protect me from the influence of evil in my life. In Jesus' name, amen.*

Listening Time

Now pray, "Holy Spirit, what are You saying to me?" Use the space provided, or a journal or notebook, to write what He reveals to you.

_____

_____

*If Jesus could have accomplished all He came
to do without fasting, why would He fast? The
Son of God fasted because He knew there
were supernatural things that could only be
released that way. How much more should
fasting be a common practice in our lives?*
—JENTEZEN FRANKLIN

Is prayer your steering wheel or your spare tire?
—ATTRIBUTED TO CORRIE TEN BOOM

*And when they had appointed elders
for them in every church, with prayer
and fasting they committed them to the
Lord in whom they had believed.*
—ACTS 14:23, ESV

CONCLUSION

As we reach the end of this twenty-one-day journey, I hope you've found not just stories and words on a page but the way to true freedom. Throughout this devotional we've explored the depths of spiritual freedom, recognizing that true freedom begins within our hearts and minds. We've seen how even those who lack physical constraints like those found in a prison can often carry invisible shackles in their souls—shackles of fear, guilt, addiction, and the like.

The key to lasting freedom lies not just in breaking free from physical or emotional bonds, walking away from the shadows of past mistakes, and stepping into the light of God's love and grace. It is found in a profound, transformative relationship with Jesus Christ. You cannot improve the gospel; it's perfect, and all we have to do is accept it!

To remain free, we must keep our focus on eternity, not the temporary. Jesus is the One who offers the truth and the way to a freedom that transcends our circumstances, a freedom that brings peace even in life's storms.

You've learned that freedom is more than a state of being; it's a journey, a continuous process of growth, learning, and surrendering to God's will. Just as the Lord instructed me to take steps along the yellow line when I was in prison, each day presents an opportunity for you to walk the narrow path, making choices that align with God's plan for your life.

Throughout these days we've explored the depths of despair, but more importantly, the heights of redemption. We've seen how the human spirit, filled with and led by the Holy Spirit, can overcome the darkest of nights and emerge into a new beginning.

I can attest that transformation doesn't happen overnight. It requires faith, perseverance, and the courage to face and overcome your inner battles. But every step forward is a step toward the person God has called you to be.

YOUR NEXT CHAPTER AWAITS

As you close this book, know that your journey doesn't end here. This is not a conclusion but a commencement. The steps you take after today will lead you toward the life you were meant to live—a life unchained, a life lived in the fullness of God's plan for you.

Embrace the path ahead with hope and determination. Let each day be a testament to the strength and resilience that lies within you as you are fueled by the Spirit of God.

Continue to pray for revelation and wisdom. Stay humble, for humility is the fertile ground in which spiritual growth thrives. Let the Holy Spirit guide you, teach you, and mold you into the image of Christ. And above all, hold on to the promise that in Jesus, your life will never be the same.

I encourage you to revisit these devotions. Whenever you feel lost or uncertain, look back to the wisdom within these pages and seek the ever-present guidance of the Holy Spirit. Reflect on your progress and keep pushing forward, even when challenges arise. Share your journey with others, for in your testimony they too may find the courage to seek their own freedom.

Embrace the truth that you are more than your past, more than your mistakes. You are a child of the King, destined for greatness and equipped for every challenge. Step forward in faith, courage, and confidence, knowing that with God all things are possible. Stop leaning on your own understanding and start trusting Him.

May your life be a testament to the power of transformation, a beacon of hope to those still walking in darkness, and a song of freedom that echoes into eternity. Your testimony is proof that the devil is a liar!

In Jesus' name, let's make this proclamation together: "My life will never be the same. I am free—truly free. The Son has set me free, so I am free indeed!"

AFTERWORD

I CAN RELATE TO the topic of this book on so many levels. I spent most of my teenage years in juvenile detention centers, and by the time I was in my twenties, I had been in and out of prison so many times it seemed like a revolving door. At the age of twenty-three, I was facing thirty years in prison on two attempted murder charges. But by the grace of God, the charges were lowered to two aggravated assaults, and I ended up serving four years of a seven-year sentence. I was twenty-seven years old when I was released and had spent most of my adult life in prison.

Back when I was incarcerated, I often imagined ways I could break out and where I would go once I was free—back to my old friends and parties, back to my family for happy reunions. But I knew I'd always have to watch my step so I didn't get caught. I used to wonder how long I could stay free. And would that really be freedom, or would it be torture knowing I was one wrong move away from being locked up again? I figured the police would eventually catch me and I'd end up back in prison with an even longer sentence.

Fortunately, I found a freedom that lasts. Because of what Christ did on the cross and the power of the Holy Spirit inside me, I am no longer a prisoner of sin, and I am no longer an inmate in a correctional facility. The freedom I now experience is not temporary but eternal.

Pastor Juan Martinez has been a mentor and friend-turned-family for years now, and one thing we both are passionate about is sharing the freedom we have found in Christ with others, including inmates who attend the prison crusades we lead together. It is truly amazing to watch Pastor Juan present the simple message of the gospel, and I am honored to collaborate with such a general on the front lines.

We always tell the inmates, "If today these prison doors were opened and each of you was told you were free to go home right now, the truth is that if you are not truly set free inside, spiritually, then physically you will be back." That is true whether you have been incarcerated or have only seen a prison on TV. There is only one path to true freedom: Jesus Christ.

Today is the day of salvation. The greatest prison break one can ever experience is passing from death unto life and having the chains of sin and bondage broken by receiving the free gift of salvation found only in Jesus Christ. (In the appendix, Juan walks you through how to accept God's free gift of salvation.) Then you have to break off the spiritual, cultural, emotional, and psychological chains that will keep you stuck, unfulfilled, and fruitless in life.

I love this book because it is a road map to that kind of freedom. You *can* be free in every area of your life—and stay free. Take this twenty-one-day journey as many times as you need for the truth in these pages to fully sink in, transform your mind, and lead you into a brighter, more fulfilling future.

—BRYANN TREJO
CHRISTIAN RAPPER
FOUNDER AND CEO, KINGDOM MUZIC

Appendix

HOW TO KNOW JESUS

Nothing in this book will work if you have not decided to make Jesus your Lord and Savior.

You may have heard people quote John 3:16—"For God so loved the world that he gave his one and only Son, that whoever believes in him shall not perish but have eternal life." But what does that mean? I like the way Rice Broocks, author of *God's Not Dead*, summarizes the gospel message: "The gospel is the good news that God became man in Jesus Christ. He lived the life we should have lived...; He then died the death we should have died...Three days later He rose from the dead, proving He is the Son of God and offering the gift of salvation to everyone who will repent and believe the gospel."[1]

It's that simple. God has already done all the work. All you must do is receive in faith the salvation God offers (Eph. 2:8–9). It's a free gift! Raising your hand at church or walking down the aisle won't save you. Surrendering your heart to Jesus Christ is the only way you can be saved.

If you want to get right with God, all you have to do is say a simple prayer like this one:

> God, I know that I have sinned against You and deserve Your wrath. But Your Son, Jesus Christ, died

on the cross in my place, taking the punishment I deserve so I could be forgiven. I confess that You are Lord. Thank You for Your grace and forgiveness— and the gift of eternal life! In Jesus' name, amen!

If you said that prayer, congratulations! Jesus asked for your hand in marriage, and you said yes. Welcome to the family of God! Making Jesus Christ the Lord of your life is by far the greatest decision you could ever make. Today is a new day for you, and you are a brand-new person in Christ. The Bible says, "Therefore, if anyone is in Christ, he is a new creation; old things have passed away; behold, all things have become new" (2 Cor. 5:17, NKJV).

Remember, it takes a lifetime to manufacture a saint. Now the work begins, but it will be worth it. Jesus is the Groom, and everything about Christianity is about becoming one with your spouse. He is in your heart, so He goes with you everywhere you go.

Begin your journey by getting connected with a body of believers, a church, and allow the Lord to order your steps by way of His Word. Read the Bible each day, meditating on it day and night, and you will be blessed in all that you do.

Accepting Christ into your heart is not behavior modification; it is a complete transformation. Your old life is gone, and a new life has begun! #PrisonBREAK

NOTES

INTRODUCTION

1. Leonardo Antenangeli, PhD, and Matthew R. Durose, "Recidivism of Prisoners Released in 24 States in 2008: A 10-Year Follow-Up Period (2008–2018)," Bureau of Justice Statistics, September 8, 2021, https://bjs.ojp.gov/library/publications/recidivism-prisoners-released-24-states-2008-10-year-follow-period-2008-2018.

DAY 1

1. Oxford Languages, s.v. "relationship," accessed April 11, 2024, https://www.google.com/search?q=relationship.
2. Oxford Languages, s.v. "relationship."

DAY 2

1. *The Burial*, directed by Maggie Betts (Culver City, CA: Amazon MGM Studios, 2023).

DAY 3

1. Michael Dye and Patricia Fancher, *The Genesis Process* (n.p.: Genesis Addiction Process & Programs, 2007), 39.
2. Dye and Fancher, *The Genesis Process*, 39.

DAY 4

1. Holman Bible Publishers, *Tony Evans Bible Commentary* (Holman Reference, 2019), 1036.

DAY 6

1. 11Alive Staff, "Hannah Payne Sentenced to Life in Prison After Following, Murdering Man Who Left Scene of Clayton County Crash," 11 Alive, December 15, 2023, https://www.11alive.com/article/news/crime/trials/hannah-payne-sentenced-murder-kenneth-herring/85-8bc93d0e-c141-457c-bb75-76b97916f68e.
2. Blue Letter Bible, s.v. *"metanoia,"* accessed April 12, 2024, https://www.blueletterbible.org/lexicon/g3341/kjv/tr/0-1/.

DAY 7

1. David Guzik, "Haggai 1—Getting Priorities Straight," Enduring Word, accessed April 11, 2024, https://enduringword.com/bible-commentary/haggai-1/.
2. Guzik, "Haggai 1—Getting Priorities Straight."

DAY 8

1. Dr. Tony Evans, "Shaking Things Up for Revival," Revive Us Again Sermon Outlines, accessed April 11, 2024, https://cdn2.hubspot.net/hub/151312/file-2347927289-pdf/docs/_Revive-Us-.

DAY 10

1. "The Pinnacle: Agape Love," Precept Austin, accessed April 11, 2024, https://www.preceptaustin.org/2_peter_16-7#love.

DAY 13

1. "Forgiveness: Your Health Depends on It," Johns Hopkins Medicine, accessed April 11, 2024,

https://www.hopkinsmedicine.org/health/wellness-and-prevention/forgiveness-your-health-depends-on-it.

2. Myles Doyle, "How Do I Forgive Someone Who's Hurt Me?," DocPlayer.net, June 8, 2014, https://docplayer.net/49842507-How-do-i-forgive-someone-who-s-hurt-me-you-asked-for-it-8-2014-am.html.

DAY 17

1. Walter A. Henrichsen, *Disciples Are Made Not Born* (Cook Communications Ministries, 1988), 40.

DAY 18

1. Charles Dickens, *A Christmas Carol* (Chapman & Hall, 1843).
2. "A Christmas Carol," Spark Notes, accessed April 11, 2024, https://www.sparknotes.com/lit/christmascarol/mini-essays/.
3. Dickens, *A Christmas Carol*.

DAY 21

1. Source unknown.

BONUS DAY

1. Encyclopedia.com, s.v. "Federal Surplus," accessed April 11, 2024, https://www.encyclopedia.com/history/dictionaries-thesauruses-pictures-and-press-releases/surplus-federal.
2. Abraham Lincoln, "Proclamation 97—Appointing a Day of National Humiliation, Fasting, and Prayer," online by Gerhard Peters and John T. Woolley, The American Presidency Project, accessed

April 11, 2024, https://www.presidency.ucsb.edu/node/203143.

APPENDIX

1. Rice Broocks, *God's Not Dead* (W Publishing Group, 2013), xvi.

ABOUT THE
Author

JUAN MARTINEZ SERVES as the senior pastor of Get Wrapped Church in Spring, Texas, and founder of Love Live Lead Ministry. Since 2010 the ministry has seen thousands of people say yes to Christ. His "heartbeat" and main focus is simply winning souls by wrapping them in the love of Christ. A true revivalist, Martinez has a burning passion to see the lost saved, the broken mended, the afflicted healed, and the body of Christ operating in its God-given authority. He speaks at conferences throughout the nation and also partners in outreaches around the United States. He has appeared on many televised programs, including TBN Salsa, TBN, CTN Vegas, JDM, *The Jim Bakker Show*, and *The Mondo Show*, and hosts a radio show and podcast called *This Is REAL*.

Martinez is the author of *Beyond the Yellow Brick Road* and co-author of the international bestseller *Imperfect Dads, One Perfect Father*. God has transformed him from having a "kill, steal, and destroy" mentality to a seed-sowing mindset, spreading the good news to all who will listen. He has seen God move miraculously in his life and longs to hear the world say, "That's crazy," as we shout, "No, that's God!"

Martinez lives in Houston with his wife, Ruthy (his Baby Ruth). They have six children: Johnathan, Jay, Jonathan, Valery, Janina, and Josh.